Java Hill:
An African Journey

A nation's evolution through
ten generations of a family
linking four continents

T.P. Manus Ulzen

Copyright © 2013 by T.P. Manus Ulzen.

Library of Congress Control Number:		2013902388
ISBN:	Hardcover	978-1-4797-9120-0
	Softcover	978-1-4797-9119-4
	Ebook	978-1-4797-9121-7

All rights reserved. No part of this book may be reproduced or transmitted in any form or by any means, electronic or mechanical, including photocopying, recording, or by any information storage and retrieval system, without permission in writing from the copyright owner.

This book was printed in the United States of America.

Rev. date: 3/19/2013

To order additional copies of this book, contact:
Xlibris Corporation
1-888-795-4274
www.Xlibris.com
Orders@Xlibris.com

Dedication

This historical account of the Ulzen family's sojourns around the world is dedicated to two men, one African and the other European. They never met and are both no longer living. Mr. Aire van Zoest, an amateur historian in Brielle, Netherlands had compiled and kept the history of one Roloef Ulsen who had been a Governor of Elmina Castle from 1755-58, because he was a family member who had achieved what appeared to be some international prominence many distant generations ago. He was aware that Roloef Ulsen had married an African woman and that all his descendants were African. He must have been the least surprised person in Brielle when my then 18 year old daughter, Adwoa Ulzen arrived from North Carolina to complete the work on the African Ulzen family tree she had been building with her father in the year following the passing of her grandfather, Edward Ulzen.

Edward Ulzen had spent most of his life as an educator and an administrator of numerous African universities. He had majored in history as an undergraduate at the University of Ghana and spent many long afternoons explaining the world to me. He was eternally enthralled by the central role of his hometown, Elmina, in world history and in the birth of Ghana as a nation. I was always intrigued by how as Africans, we had come by the surname Ulzen. I understood this in general terms, because there were many Elminians with Dutch names from the 3 centuries of Dutch presence in the old city-state.

The best oral history available from my father was that of a distant ancestor named Hermanus van Ulzen who had been an administrator of sorts at Elmina Castle, generations ago. This was the extent of my knowledge of the origins of my surname until he passed on the family documents to me the year before he died.

What struck me most in the intermittent research which grew into this book was the desire with which both men, African and European, held onto the information they had, having faith that eventually the whole story would be joined.

My father went to the village on October 1, 1999 and I was informed of the passing of Aire van Zoest in 2004 by his cousin Frederika Wardner Gilroy in Vermont with whom I had established correspondence after the European and African wings of the family became aware of each other through the research leading to the whole story.

This book is dedicated to the long evening conversations that Edward and Aire never had on an Elmina veranda. Maybe, they have now had their conversations and united their story.

T. P. Manus Ulzen

Gratitude

I must express my deepest appreciation to many individuals who read this manuscript at various stages of its development. First I thank my wife Ekua and children Adwoa, Kweku and Kofi, who have endured a decade of the ups and downs of "the book". I must single out my daughter Adwoa as my principal collaborator in this project and thank her for her unvarnished input through the process.

My thanks also go to Prof. Sekyi-Otu who thoroughly reviewed the manuscript, along with Prof. Molara Ogundipe who tired of my misuse of commas. Finally, Dr. Boatemaa Boateng also provided very useful qualitative insights which helped me finally unveil this book to the reading public.

There are many others; including Dr. Ineke van Kessel, University of Leiden, who searched for and provided me with much archival information which encouraged me on this writing journey. In essence, she brought the story to me. Dr. Michel Doortmont, University of Gronigen and Dr. Natalie Everts, University of Leiden were also similarly helpful with information they provided.

Dr. Kwadwo Opoku - Agyeman, University of Cape Coast, also provided me with useful feedback after reading the manuscript.

There are also many members of the extended family my brother Edward included, who provided and sought clarifications on parts of the family history and good friends who have truly encouraged me along the way. I am eternally grateful.

I

He stood on the northern balcony of the castle overlooking the town. It was much larger than a balcony, a large open space with a few cannons looking over the town. He looked out and wondered about last night, thinking, "Was it the right thing to do?" The town was unusually calm, and there was an uneasy quiet in the castle too. He was about five feet eight inches tall with a moustache of authority. His wig was in place, shielding his graying and thinning red hair. He was after all, governor of this castle and he thought, "of Elmina too!" Governor Hogenboom, the fifty-ninth governor of Elmina Castle, had done what no predecessor of his had done before. He had fired cannons into the town. It doesn't matter why he did it. It is the fact that he did it that made him muse.

He went out as he usually did in the evening to visit some of his compatriots as he did on ordinary days. He walked back from Niezer's Garden alone in this now very peaceful town. But it had always been a peaceful town. In an instant his very life left his consciousness. Dead! Hogenboom is gone. The governor lies on a dusty road. His immaculate whites browned with the dark earth of Africa. The governor is dead. No, killed. Yes, killed. He did what no other had done before him. Fired cannons into the town. A peaceful town but a strong town with pride and very strong feelings.

Our Elmina is a sleepy and peaceful ancient town with a quiet yet lively temperament, resting on the Atlantic shore. The waves are boisterous, and the sea is red with rage on many days. At other times it is an ever-peaceful blue dotted with men young and old, sailing in their canoes. The waves always hit the shore with emphasis, as if to say this land belongs to the sea! Its anger might be directed at the sun, which shines relentlessly, reflecting short shadows without permission over the waters of the Atlantic. The ocean roars loudly at this old city-state, but the people are deaf to its centuries' old stories of hope, promise, tragedy, and triumph through its various transformations. The ocean is Elmina; we live on the land but the ocean is the home of the city and its history. We call our town Edina but it has been known to the world as Elmina (*El Mina*—the mine) ever since white men seeking gold arrived here.

From the main street, running from east to west, the only destination is the castle, easily the largest edifice of the town. Architecturally, it looks at the town, dwarfing all others except for the three hills that stand north of it. Directly across the river is St. Jago Hill and east of that, across the Benya River, is Java Hill. Further north and west is St. Joseph's Hill, on top of which, stands the Catholic Church peering over the whole town. The bridge over the Benya River welcomes the castle, and the street turns north and west through Bantama, the African soul of Elmina. This was the site of the old city before its history of reluctantly accepting cannon balls on fire caused it to spread in haste across the river to the east. The road then runs rapidly through the community of fishermen who are the keepers of Elmina's African heritage. It passes west then north back to the main highway leading west to Takoradi and east to Cape Coast and eventually Accra, the capital of Ghana. This city, teeming with black Africans fishing, trading, laughing, cluttering the streets, gives few clues about its own story. It sits at the center of how this country became a nation. In 1859, Elmina had a population of 39,899 and was the largest coastal settlement of local Africans in the Gold Coast. Accra, the present day capital of Ghana had a population of only 14,865. Butri was the second largest town, home to 15,700 inhabitants. What then are the stories hidden in the waves of the ocean, on the hilltops of Elmina, and in the walls of the castle? What will Elmina tell us of herself and about ourselves? Is it a state, a town, or a fishing village; and how has its past brought us here?

One hundred and fifty yards from the bridge to the castle sits the

Methodist church. The streets cut a lively isosceles triangle around it, along with beaten down honking taxis, hawkers, and ordinary folk. The cardinal point leads toward the Dutch cemetery beyond the No. 4 Posuban Shrine. At the shrine, you take a left, and fifty yards or so down the road, now overtaken by dust disguising the ancient asphalt, stands the now very aged Aacht family house still in great shape. The ever present Ghanaian gutter demarcates the street from the house. I step over two scraggly cement blocks, walk on the wide concrete pavement, greet the tenants downstairs and ask if "master" is upstairs. They nod, say so, and point up all at once. I run up eight wooden ladderlike steps on the almost vertical incline, a sharp left through the partition, and I am in Mr. Mensah's sitting room. This, no more than a ten by ten-foot space, is an odd pentagon of a room. The linoleum is old: edges bitten and battle-weary, straining to cover the floor. A few lean cats hesitate about whether to leave or stay and we begin with *amanee* (the news). I present him with a bottle of European liquor, and he says, "You are most welcome!" I'm never sure if the greeting is meant for the bottle he caresses ever so gently or me.

The news of our journey to this place always grows into history of the family itself. Now at seventy, Mr. Mensah, a retired school principal still looks young and sprightly but moves carefully as he responds to his true age and our amanee. He always expresses his disappointment about how the illustrious sons and daughters of the family have neglected the house. This is a pet peeve of his. He is otherwise quite a nostalgic and friendly man. He is about six feet tall obviously graying but a trim 175 pounds for his height.

He gives me a run down on the health status of all his cousins across the street at *Akodee Turo Mu* where their maternal family house is located. In all my life, I have been up those steps no more than ten times, and that is a generous count. This cat-colonized room, simple, in need of paint to show off its beautiful colonial furniture, is where I believe my father's soul rests. If indeed, it does rest on this earth. Cousin George was easily my father's favorite relation. He was his nephew though only three years younger than him. Through the *amanee*, George explains his closeness to his Ulzen cousins. He tells me that his mother died soon after his birth and that as an infant, my father's mother nursed him along with her own baby Wilhelmina.

Artist impression of Ships at Elmina in 1629

II

On this bright Sunday morning after an unusually early cold beer sitting in the great room of the Conduah home, the guests were already in a merry mood, and the chatter was as joyous as one would find on a market day anywhere in West Africa. I had come to Elmina again within a week to lend support to my sister's celebration of the tenth anniversary of her mother's passing. It was an elaborate feast. The guests had just returned from the cemetery where they unveiled the commemorative plaque, said prayers, and hoped the gods would absolve them of their foibles. We were late because we stopped to see our guests from the Netherlands who were at the Oyster Bay Hotel, a rather modest seaside resort just east of the town. The historian Dr. Van Kessel, whose work had brought us all together, had apparently broken her ankle while taking pictures on Java Hill with Mr. and Mrs. Cordus, the Indonesian descendants of African soldiers who had fought and lived on Java in the 1800s. Now in their seventies, the Corduses had made their first pilgrimage to Ghana knowing that their grandparents had sailed to the Dutch East Indies from Elmina.

My sister, Angelina and I, were with her two-year-old daughter, Mubie, when we went to see Dr. Van Kessel and the Corduses. The good historian seemed comfortable enough in her suite. The plaster of Paris was barely hanging on the leg, which housed the fractured bone. She rested her injured foot on an ordinary chair. This mishap had immobilized this very active and high-spirited woman, but only physically though, for she was still a picture of excitement and curiosity. Angelina and I looked at the grainy x-rays and were comforted that it was a non-displaced fracture of the fibula. The half cast on her foot looked rather weak, but it would have to survive until she made it back to the Netherlands in a week. As long as she bore no weight on it, all would be well. Her crutches rested patiently against the wall and the relentless roar of the powerful waves of the mighty Atlantic.

As a result of this house call, we got to the cemetery only to realize that the first portion of the commemoration had ended. We followed the last car in the departing convoy to the family house at the end of the procession and rolled into the Lorry Park adjacent to the house just east of the Methodist church. The Lorry Park has the unlikely moniker of Chapel Square. We alighted from the vehicle and immediately enjoyed familiar, hearty, and long greetings with those arriving and colliding with us. It was indeed a bright morning, and the smells of the day had not yet peaked. It was warm but still comfortable. Almost everybody was dressed in a blue-and-white fabric denoting mourning tempered with joy. Ten years after the fact, there was more white than blue.

We worked our way through the wall of neighborhood children who were gathered around the large loud speakers at the foot of the wide majestic but aged wooden stairs leading to the great room upstairs. The children were waiting for many things: an act of kindness, usually money, for the music to start, and often for whatever food or candy would fall from the bounty of the celebrants upstairs. We made it up the stairs, stopping many times to greet and be greeted. Finally, the threshold opened into a narrow corridor. The kitchen and all the sweet smells of the hard work from days and nights before greeted us invitingly from the right. Our stomachs were ready for the seduction that lay ahead. The great room itself was to the left. There were people everywhere. The men were mostly in traditional cloths, mainly blue and white in color; and the women, though faithful to the colors, presented a wide spectrum of designs from traditional to western. I gave a customary wave to the right to acknowledge those seated close to the kitchen as we worked our way to the left, toward the great room through the heavily inhabited corridor. We negotiated our way through the great room by greeting those already seated from right to left in an counter clockwise manner as custom dictates. After about thirty minutes of these procedural maneuvers, we were ready to soothe our souls.

Johanna, my oldest paternal cousin, a teacher and self-declared pauper who was always in a good mood, was engaged in her perpetual worries about her children but expressed her usual romantic views of the family and its rapidly disappearing greatness.

Madam Adwoa Sekyi and her cousin Mansa Mensah were also in that corner right next to the source of oncoming gustatory excitement, a white draped table at the west end of the room. Above the table hung an elegant black-and-white sketched portrait of Chief Conduah in the full western attire of a nineteenth-century gentleman. He looked satisfied. I wondered what it was like in his day. Were the celebrations bigger? What did they talk about then? I wondered.

I walked across the Lorry Park, a little out of place in my black suit. There were the usual waves, nods, and courtesies. As I hit the No. 4 Posuban Shrine, I made a left turn for the first time on foot, for I had always made the trip by car with my father. I looked up and could see Mr. Mensah in his window. It took all of three minutes to find myself in his crammed living room. The cats found their way out, and we abridged our *amanee* as we had been together only a week before to unveil my father's tomb.

In his large Bermuda shorts *sans* shirt, he said he felt well. He dispelled all the concerns from the women in the family about his health and, of course, his love of liquor. He reassured me that the customary bottle of whisky I had greeted him with barely a week before would cause him no harm. After all, the gods were to share in it. He was extremely happy with the restraint we had shown in dealing with the head of their family, his older cousin and a brilliant legal mind but with a reputation in the family as a super litigant. My old cousin's failing eyesight had made him wonder who the man in the black suit may have been. For a moment, he thought it was my father. He was sure it was he, and then as I got closer, he was assured it was a living man and not a ghost. He was almost breathless by the time I got upstairs. I had not planned to perturb him with my farewell visit. He began to cry. I know he prayed that this would not be the last goodbye, so wished I. We wished each other well with that firm handshake that is a lie when your soul is stressed with the fear of an ending.

I had seen those tears and felt that strong handshake from his uncle, my father, just over a year before, as I sat with him in his private room at the 37 Military Hospital in Accra before I caught my flight back to the United States. His illness was coming gradually to an end and with it his life. And what a life it had been. He had thin tears of inevitability in his eyes and spoke gratitude to me in a manner too heavy to bear. It was surreal—just the two of us, father and son, the old and young, the dying generation and the growing one. We shook hands firmly. I placed my left hand over his right shoulder to draw him closer, but he stood up like a soldier, at attention to his son, now an officer to preside over his life as it faded into the beginning of his eternity. It was an uneasy dawn for me that night; a new era without a leader. We had just finished taping what would be his last video broadcast to his children and grandchildren. He wished me a safe trip with thanks. I dissuaded him from his repetitive expressions of gratitude, but he insisted with a frightening finality. In his white singlet and his striped pajama pants, he was as always a model of modesty, integrity, elegant simplicity, and basic humanity. This was the last time our eyes met.

The weeks to follow were indeed terrible; our phone conversations became too labored for him. For a man who loved conversation above all else, they became too short. On Thursday, September 30, 1999, during our last conversation, sensing my worry, he said, "I am not dead yet." He was trying helplessly to protect me from the inevitable. It was his final parental act discharged with grace and characteristic care.

Why did he love Elmina so? He grew up here, and I knew he was happiest visiting his aging relatives, asking of their well-being and always giving them something to lighten life's load and cheer them up. He was generous to a fault, and as his cousin George said of him, "The poor have lost a great friend in Elmina. He had it (money) and he shared it." He was not a wealthy man by any measure, but he recognized the poverty around him all his life and did what he could to soften its hard blows on the many who were unhappily married to it.

Mr. George Amoakwa Mensah of the Nyanyiwa Family looking through his window at the Aacht House in Elmina (2000)

St Joseph's Catholic Church in Elmina

III

I enjoyed the music of the mass immensely, and it drew me deeper into my own soul. From the driveway around St. Joseph's Catholic Church, plateaued atop the hill, I looked westward over the town at St. Jago and at Java Hill not knowing that my eyes were telling me where the story truly began. A year ago, we had been here to complete that heavy task of saying goodbye to Nanabanyin Edward Abraham Ulzen. During the mass, the announcer hailed him as "a great man of Africa" as we were dancing the Friday-borns to victory during the "Kofi and Ama" collection at the end of the mass. On that occasion, I felt compelled to take a picture of St. Jago and Java Hill from the only other peak in the city, St. Joseph's Catholic Church where the Ulzens had worshipped for well over a century.

In my time, I was close to Elmina only twice. These two periods were between the ages of ten and twelve, when I attended my father's alma mater, St. Augustine's College in Cape Coast and in 1979, when I worked as a physician at Cape Coast Regional Hospital.

I remember one visit from my father particularly vividly. It was one to St. Augustine's; an unexpected one in which he was accompanied by his older brother, Uncle Jacob. Jacob was an ebullient man, a large man in my eyes. He was my father's big brother. He stood tall with his bulging prominent eyes playing with my every move. He was an active observer as father and son tried to make a visit last longer than the school rules permitted. They didn't drive into the school but parked on the main road alongside the toothless barrier that failed to keep us on campus. Someone was sent for me, and I walked across the detention field toward the two of them. They were already hearty when I arrived. I was surprised by the circumstances but happy that my financial position could only improve. Jacob was unmarried then, and the two brothers seemed ecstatic just to be together. Jacob was the headmaster of the Catholic school in Elmina and was also the choirmaster of St. Joseph's Catholic Church. He died probably no more than two years after this joyous meeting. My father was also a musician and had been a choirmaster wherever he lived, in Kumasi, Lusaka, Maseru, and in Nairobi in my own memory. The Ulzens of my day loved a good drink. They also loved to sing, read, challenge the facts, laugh heartily, attend mass, and play the piano.

IV

In 1979, one of my favorite Ulzen aunts was visiting Elmina from her home in Tema. I heard she was in Elmina for a few days. At that time, I was working in Cape Coast, only ten miles or so to the east. I got into my little military green Datsun and headed down westward to see her on that fine Saturday morning. My aunt Joanna Codjoe had been widowed a year earlier and was in Elmina to partake in the traditional rights, which freed her as a woman from her deceased husband. The funeral of her husband in Cape Coast a year earlier had been a rather dramatic affair. When I arrived at Mr. Codjoe's family house, his son, my cousin tossed a package tied in a handkerchief to me as I was alighting from a taxi and motioned to me to keep moving. I caught it and told the driver to step on it. And as I proceeded toward the town hall, I realized that tied in the handkerchief were the bolts to the tires of his father's car. Apparently, his father's relatives had made a move to inherit the car by force. Without the bolts, the tires were useless; and the car could not move, at least for a while.

Auntie Joanna was easily the most devout Catholic in the family, at least as I saw it. She had made a recent pilgrimage to Rome and seemed quite fulfilled for having done this. We sat downstairs in the little veranda at the south end of my grandfather's house facing the Atlantic Ocean. She looked well, and her spirits were good. She had always looked on the heavier side, as many of my aunts did. She was dressed in a slightly dark traditional

Java wax print. She said she was somewhat unhappy about any traditional African rights, which could be in conflict with her strong Catholic beliefs and practice but didn't dwell much on this. She teased me about rumors of my impending marriage and gave me a healthy dose of motherly advice. She was quite heartened that I was about to walk with leaden feet. My carefree days were soon to be over.

Later that night, I was nursing a cold beer with two friends at our watering hole in Cape Coast when an acquaintance entered. On seeing me he said, "Do you know that your aunt is dead?" "No, which one?" I responded. "Mrs. Codjoe," he intoned. I was possessed with disbelief. "That cannot be." The warm effect of the cold Star beer was rapidly evaporating as an icy shiver took over my body and my being, in the dark of the hot tropical night. "I was with her all day today, and she was quite well." The doctor in me insisted. I found myself speeding down the ocean front highway driving westward from the Texaco beer bar. I zoomed over the lagoon, taking in its stench and wondering if it had some healing properties. The ocean on my left as I drove seemed suddenly darker and louder and more foreboding than it had ever been. It was now sinister. I would soon pass St. Augustine's College, my alma mater, and the Methodist school and then found myself within minutes at the entrance to Cape Coast University. It is amazing how fast one travels in a situation, which is irreversible. I swung left and further west, and because there was little traffic, I zoomed through the fishing villages and was at Iture in no time. I still could not believe that this was possible.

"She died suddenly after she got to Accra," I was told after I walked around to the back of the house. A few neighbors, who had already gathered, were sitting on benches in and around the veranda. The ocean continued to rage louder than usual. The breeze was thin and the air was heavy. It was apparently a heart attack. All too sudden.

V

Her funeral was the first at the Ulzen household I was old enough to attend and observe with some interest. My future wife's family had paid a preliminary visit to the Ulzen house just before my aunt died, to acknowledge that my maternal uncle had officially made it known to them that he had an interest in their family. This meant that I had officially informed my family of my plans to marry their daughter and they had been so informed. The timing was awful as the Ulzens could not consider the process of meetings about the impending marriage and a funeral at the same time. Everything came to a tense and impatient yet understanding standstill for me. I was getting ready to leave for Canada as my postgraduate plans had become clearer. The need and desire to accomplish everything before I left was rapidly mounting.

According to Akan custom, the maternal family of the dead person has ownership of the body, for that is the person's true lineage and family. At the wake, keeping the maternal family of the Ulzens, the Nyanyiwa family, was at the center of everything. It seemed nothing could be achieved without their assent. Papa Mensah, the headmaster's older brother and the *Ebusuapanyin* or head of the family, and his entourage arrived from *Akodaa Turo Mu* amid the usual crying, praying, and general cacophony present at these large gatherings. The throng had gathered from all over the neighborhood. She was lying in state in what used to be her father, P.

M. Ulzen's, living room upstairs; and well-wishers, curiosity seekers, and others were filing past after negotiating the steep wooden staircase. At one point, her body had to be lifted and moved downstairs to be placed in the coffin. It was a logistical nightmare. My cousins, Papa Annan and Francisca, had become orphans in one very short year. Again, the beer wore off rapidly as I realized that my older cousin, Francis Ulzen-Appiah; the now orphaned Papa Annan; and myself were the only young men of note around. My father, the only surviving male, was in India on a consultancy, completely unaware of the events of this night. I wished he were there, not because she was heavy, for he would not have helped lift her. He had an aversion to physical exertion. He loved her so and took a great interest in her melancholia-tormented life. She was prone to episodes of deep depression, and I was always impressed with how her sisters, Wilhelmina and Mary, shared her care when she was ill.

After some bickering between the elders and the restating of centuries-old slights, mistreatments, and bad memories between the nuclear and extended family, the job was done. We transported her carefully downstairs into the box that was to be her final earthly home. There was a clear resentment by the *Ebusua* or maternal family about having to conduct the proceedings at my aunt's paternal home. I knew not why then.

At this time of interment, when you expect people to let go of old problems, they ironically disinter and magnify old peeves and settle old scores. I later learned, after tongues were loosened by anger, drink, and music that my grandfather, Patrick Manus Ulzen, a man renowned for his high voltage temper, had gone nuclear on his wife's family during her terminal illness which had led to her death in 1950 at the age of fifty-five.

Legend has it that he informed the Nyanyiwa family that his wife, their royal princess, was very ill and that they needed to visit her as often as they could because her condition was grave. Supposedly, he was dissatisfied with what he considered to be a measure of disinterest on the part of her family, his in-laws. So when she did pass away, he reportedly sent a delegation, as required by custom, to inform the Nyanyiwa family of the expected but truly tragic event as she was the eighth of her mother's nine children. The ninth, Kwamena Sope, had been long deceased. The following day, they returned the visit as required by tradition. He was reportedly in no mood to be hospitable.

The houses at this compound in Sybil, Elmina, are arranged in a U shape with the open end facing the main street and the ocean about eighty yards south of the house. The Ulzen house is at the apex or closed end of the U. It is said that, as the Nyanyiwa delegation made their way from the street to the house, he reportedly exhorted his neighbors to hoot at and heckle the arriving delegation. Legend has it that after his men heckled the delegation, he informed them that since they had shown little interest in his wife's condition, in her death, they had forfeited the right to claim her body as their own. He reportedly announced that he would take care of all the final arrangements himself and that if they wished to attend the funeral, it would be at his home. He went ahead with his plans.

Nattily dressed in his three-piece suit as usual, he made his way to the post office where he sent out telegrams to each of their children, who at that time were not living in Elmina. He laid her in state in the matrimonial home and handled the funeral arrangements. I have no doubt that his wife's family was not saddened by his own passing seven years later. The death of Angelina Aikins a.k.a. Mrs. Angelina Ulzen set the precedent for her children being laid in state at their paternal home instead of their mother's family home. This is why there was grief beyond the loss of a dear, kind woman expressed at my Aunt Joanna's funeral. The mountain of the extended family had to come to the Mohammed of the nuclear family, an entity for which no word exists in any Akan language.

My aunt Joanna's Requiem mass was packed with mourners and others at St. Joseph's Catholic Church. Her devout connection to her religion spoke volumes of her life. I spent most of the funeral mass outside of the building, standing with one of my cousins as His Grace, the archbishop of Cape Coast, the late J. K. Amissah, a close family friend, commanded her soul "to the angels in paradise." It was a bright and sunny morning with all the colors of Elmina in full bloom. It was a good day to formally leave this earthly life.

I wondered who Auntie Nana Kraba, as she was known at home, had been named after; and no one could give me a clear answer.

Home of Patrick Manus Ulzen in Sybil, Elmina (in 1999)

Patrick Manus Ulzen and his family (1939). Edward
A. Ulzen, age 13 is 2nd from left back row.

VI

Our family name, Ulzen, had caused me some moments of questioning; so at every opportunity, I sought clues to its origin. Outside a few coastal places like Elmina, Sekondi, or Axim, it was not known. It was a Dutch name, which in Elmina was not unusual. European names were not uncommon in coastal towns. Black folk with white names were to be had two a penny along the coast.

In the '70s, with liberation struggles abounding in Africa and being an active member of the Student Movement for African Unity myself, I was somewhat discomfited by the sense that I had a name that was part of the colonial legacy. Many people with similar European names had adopted African ones to strengthen their credentials as revolutionaries. For some, it was easy because their European names were simply corruptions of well-known African names. Others had African names they could fall back on in their paternal line. Not me. My "home name" was Papa Mends after my grandfather. This was hardly an African name in this time of great existential angst!

Many people with names like ours were either light-skinned or had light-skinned relatives a generation or two away, which clued you in on the recent European origins of the name. I knew no light-skinned Ulzens though I later heard of some in Sekondi. We were all dark or of average

African complexion. So at times, I wondered if a distant African ancestor, to advance himself on the Europeanized coast, adopted this name.

One July afternoon in 1974, my father and I were together at home in Maseru, the capital of Lesotho. As we reflected on life over a few lagers, I asked him about the name and what he knew about its origins. He said it was Dutch in origin, and as far as he knew, the original Dutch ancestor was called Hermanus van Ulsen or Hulsen. He said that over time, it had become Ulzen, which was more consistent with the pronunciation in the Fanti language, which is replete with Z sounds. As far as he knew, Hermanus worked in some administrative capacity with the Dutch at the castle. He was surer of the ownership of the name than I could have been in my revolutionary African world at the University of Ghana where the only European name with status was Guevara! He dissuaded me from changing it by saying, "Your name is your history. That is your story."

He planned to research it when he had more time, probably by the next eclipse of the sun! He had little time for such luxuries. When I was baptized as Thaddeus Patrick Manus-Ulzen; he added Manus to my surname to keep the original name alive. I returned to plain Ulzen to fit in with everyone else.

This name caused me other grief as time went on. I had to spell it at every turn. This was invariably followed with "What kind of name is that?" It attempted to deny me some of my birthrights from time to time.

At the University of Ghana, we referred to our allowance of thirty-two cedis a semester as "the millions." Well, the millions were adjusted upward for inflation after one powerful antigovernment demonstration paralyzed the military government in 1974. It was increased to one hundred cedis per semester with back pay. I am sure that inflation was only part of the story. The weight of one hundred cedis in the hands of each student was meant to extinguish any residual anti-government sentiments that we harbored. I arrived at the administrative offices at Legon Hall to pick up my share of the national cake.

"Name?"

"'Ulzen'"

"'Huh?'"

"Ulzen. U-L-Z-E-N, Ulzen," I declared, getting louder.

He looked at me up and down, sideways, and backwards if he could, in a split second. He opened a ledger that held the secret to the millions for deserving citizens. "Hmmm, are you a Ghanaian?"

"Yes, absolutely," I said, getting angry.

"Your address it is in uhh… " "The Kingdom of Lesotho," I said, becoming sarcastically more formal. Before he could continue on that path, I went on quickly, "My father was a student here, you know?" I said, calming down a bit. "Yeah, what year?"

"He finished in 1956; he was one of the first one hundred. He was the first occupant of S 24." "Hey, okay," he said, calling his older officemate. "Have you heard this name before? Horison."

"No."

"Where are you from?"

"Elmina. *Me fe Edina,*" I said in Fanti.

"Ahh, now I understand," he said with a smirk. "Okay, we will arrange for you to get your money… uhhh let me see… Tuesday." "Okay, we will see you Tuesday, Mr. Horison." "Thank You."

At the next near denial of my birthright, I was not present. It was only reported to me by my then girlfriend, now my wife. I had applied with a good friend, Ernest Nortey, for a scholarship to fund our elective studies in the UK from the Akotex Foundation. Apparently, they were okay with Nortey's application; but they wondered, "Is this other one, Ulzen, a Ghanaian?" Luckily for me, my prospective father-in-law, Professor A. Mensah, was a board member and said, "Oh yes. You know, E. A. Ulzen, the former registrar of the Kwame Nkrumah University?" Then sudden recognition. "Yes, yes. Edward, yes." We were funded, in any case, by GIHOC Pharmaceuticals and DANAFCO so it was only an academic issue at the time.

My last nomenclature game actually worked in my favor. I was traveling with my daughter and son and stopped over in Frankfurt en route to Toronto where we lived. We were enjoying one of those exciting long waits at the airport when the voice on the public address system said, "Vould zee Doktor Ooltzen pleaze come to zee counter?" When I got there, this German fellow was perplexed. "Are you Doktor Ooltzen?" "Yes, indeed," I said with my black face. There was a twin pregnant pause. "Okay. Vee are overbooked, zo I vould like to upgrade you to business class, do you have a problem wiz zat?"

"Absolutely not, sir."

Some hesitation, then, "If you don't mind"—I knew it was coming—"Where are you from?"

"I was born in Ghana, West Africa," I said. "This is a Dutch name."

"Also eet eez here in Germany."

"Yes, I know, the Dutch were in Elmina, my home town for 264 years; and we also had the Brandenburgers, but they didn't stay as long. You know they left a lot of children there."

I couldn't tell if he cringed or shuddered, but he was red just the same and let out a little squeaky laugh. "Have a good flight." "My children too?" "Oh yes, yes, all of you. Thank you, Dr. Ooltzen."

Author's mother, Mrs. Christiana Ulzen (nee Andrews)
at Holy Child Training College circa 1954

E. A. Ulzen as a Graduate Student at
The University of Ghana 1956

VII

When my father turned seventy, I didn't make a trip to Ghana, and none of his other four children did. We were all caught up in the daily grind of the rat race, which was in any event being won by the rats. We phoned in our congratulations, and he seemed to have recovered so well from his heart attacks suffered three years before, so complacency had settled into our minds and hearts. I was sure I would make it for his seventy-fifth birthday. It never came. He died in his seventy-fourth year.

In 1998, my uncle-in-law died after a brief illness, and my wife and her whole family left from Toronto for his funeral at Saltpond in Ghana. Everyone who saw my father at Mr. Arhin's funeral reported in glowing terms how well he looked. My wife actually had a beautiful photograph to prove it. She urged me to visit him, and for once, I let go of my schedule and took one week off just to visit my father. I stayed at a friend's in the suburbs of Accra and visited him at his home in Kaneshie every day I was there.

One early evening, the two of us walked down his little street to visit a neighbor about a block away. He was a retired fellow civil servant who was recuperating from prostate surgery. As we walked down Palace Close toward the "Mother's Inn" junction, an acquaintance shouted harmlessly to him, "Nana, is this your son?"

"No! I am not old enough to have such an old man for a son." He was wedded to youth, and we believed he would truly stay forever young.

That evening, it was rather cool and the air was only ever so slightly in breeze. We pulled two chairs and sat in front of the water tank at the back of his house. We exchanged tidbits of news, and as always, we shared our dreams. He loved to converse more than he loved to sing, teach, or act; most of all, he liked to laugh. He said, as the conversation veered toward my contemporaries in government, "You know Ato Austin? He's dead." I responded, "Yeah, he died about a year or so ago, not so?" He looked at me over his glasses, showing that I did not get it. "Not my Ato Austin," referring to Master Austin, another venerable Elmina educator. "His son, *your* Ato Austin. His son, the minister." "What? Last time I was here, he was one of the people I bumped into at the arrivals hall at Kotoka Airport." "Paa Kwesi, bring all of last week's *Daily Graphic*!" He went through the pile of newspapers and fished out the issue reporting the sad news of this brilliant, young officer of the government. Another flame extinguished as we traveled in unknown lands. I was cold.

I sipped my beer to wipe it all away. The maneuver did not work well this time. The news sat like an elephant on my chest. I simply could not believe it. He took a careful swig of his water as his heart had retired him from all of life's pleasures except prayer, conversation, and hearty laughter. He segued into this thing about himself and his father. They had been estranged for some time, mostly about his choice of my mother as a wife. Old Patrick Manus Ulzen had tried to get Archbishop Porter to caveat the marriage unsuccessfully. His second daughter, Elizabeth, had married Robert Adjaye-Fraiku, my mother's uncle. It appears, for his own reasons, he did not approve of a second marriage between the two families. He didn't want my father to marry another from the Bantuma royal family. My Mother, Christiana Andrews, was his son-in law's niece from the De Heer family in Elmina. Her father was John Andrews, a mulatto surveyor from Cape Coast of English descent. My mother had the will to match P. M. Ulzen, and he didn't take kindly to that. She was one of the few people on the surface of the earth who could go toe-to-toe with him. She was a working woman and didn't take bull from anyone. She still doesn't, though we can now say no to her.

My father was in Kumasi when he got word his father was seriously ill and had been admitted to Cape Coast Hospital. This was in 1962. He found his father in a stable state, having suffered a heart attack a few days earlier. They had a very good conversation; his father expressed his pride of him, saying, "I understand the president has given you a big post in Kumasi." Satisfied with their new rapprochement, he bade his father goodbye, promising to visit the following week. He died on a Monday night, and on Tuesday morning, all his Asafo men from the No. 7 Company were in Elmina, on terra firma and not on the high seas. This was so because on Tuesdays fishermen do not visit the sea. It is the sea's day of rest. The men in Elmina, as in many Fanti coastal societies, are organized in volunteer militias which traditionally formed the local army in bygone years. These militias are called companies. There are ten in Elmina. My grandfather, P. M. Ulzen, was the captain of No. 7 Company. He had promised his militiamen for many years that he'd fall dead on a Tuesday, their day off, in jest and in defiance.

One night, during my visit to see my father in 1998, I asked a few questions about the family as the night wore on. The night was bright as the sky was alight with shining stars. It was a timeless period, as my father began to tell me that he envied one of his friends, late Mr. Joseph Hubster Yorke (father of Ghanaian politician and business leader, Dr. Kwesi Nduom), who had died suddenly, almost effortlessly. He wished for an exit like Master Yorke's. He didn't want to wither into dependency, having others turn and toilet him. This was a fate worse than death itself, he believed. He wanted to be called quickly. For the first time, I saw in his voice the picture of death's inevitability and his readiness to face it. I was comforted by his calm and serenity about this. There was even a hint of courage, ever so fleeting.

He explained that his father had no brothers in Ghana. The Ulzens in Sekondi were descendants of his father's cousins, not his brothers' children as I had always assumed. My great grandfather, Jacob A. F. Ulzen, at first a Dutch and later a British Customs official, was first stationed in Ghana and later in Calabar, Nigeria. He had retired to Elmina, and upon his death, all his children arrived from Calabar to bury him. My grandfather, the younger son, remained and settled in Elmina even though everyone returned to Calabar except his younger sister Adina, whose house is behind the Ulzen house in Sybil. She's the mother of the Affuls. My father's cousin, Mr. Afful, had died just a few years before my father had returned to Ghana upon his retirement. He had often spoken about how he had planned to spend time with him again in their golden years. They had worked together in Kumasi in the early sixties at Kwame Nkrumah University of Science and Technology (KNUST).

He mentioned with interest that he hoped I could track down the Calabar line of the family someday. That evening he handed me copies of the birth records of all of his siblings and also a typewritten sheet with a list of his father's brothers and sisters and a quotation from his grandfather, J. A. F. Ulzen, on the sad occasion of his wife Elizabeth Asorbu Ulzen's death. I tried to postpone the acquisition of these documents, but he was insistent that I keep them.

The quotation from his grandfather read:

> "On the memorable morning of January 24th 1910, Mrs. Elizabeth Ulzen alias Adjuah Asorbu, passed away triumphantly after a protracted illness, amidst universal grief and tears of a genuine nature. Her surviving children with their aged father most deeply declare the loss an unbearable one but are warmly comforted in the fact that she sleeps peacefully in Jesus, waiting for resurrection morning. Born January 24th 1858 she was in the 52nd year when the inevitable hand of death claimed her to that happy place where sorrow and trouble are no more. May his holy will be done".

Jacob A. F. Ulzen died on July 13, 1910.

E A Ulzen as Safohen (Captain or Vaandrig of no. 7 Asafo Company at Edina *Bronya* 1979)

Edward Ulzen at funeral of Mr. Ebenezer Arhin (Nanabanyin VII) (The author's uncle in law) in Saltpond (1998)

Inauguration of Board of Bureau of Ghanaian Languages
with Edward Ulzen 3rd from left, as Chairman (1998)

VIII

This had been a hectic week in May 1998. I took time out from visiting my father in Accra to visit my maternal grandmother in Tarkwa, as I did religiously on every visit to Ghana. I spent a day visiting my maternal relatives in Takoradi. In Akan, life obligations to your maternal relatives are taken seriously. They are my family and will be responsible for me when I can no longer speak for myself.

Before this, I had stopped in Elmina, visiting the Ulzen house in Sybil. My aunt Yacoba was clearly aging rapidly. This small mild-mannered woman was the oldest of my father's siblings. Her memory was not hers anymore; she could hardly walk, and the stress on her only daughter Johanna and the older grandchildren was etched in their demeanor and conversation.

My father, in his usual effort to generate hope, gave me a walking stick, which he said had belonged to his father. He asked me to give it to his sister in Elmina. I presented it to her along with a few bags of Fanti *kenkey*, which I had bought as usual at Yamoransa on my way to Elmina. I then also paid a call to Mrs. Tetteh, my mother's aunt who to my surprise had lost all her vision. My mind traveled back to the days in the sixties when she managed the KNUST Elmina Motel. This is now the site of Elmina Beach Resort Hotel. I would visit from St. Augustine's for assured pampering for my little soul. Those were times so young, so bright, so rich, and so alive. Life was oh so perfect!

I walked back toward the car and the driver Mr. Osei, who read my face correctly, asked, "It was bad here too, heh?" The family was vanishing slowly, and I was enveloped by a heavy sense of helplessness as I felt the living history of these wonderful people slipping away. Mrs. Christina Tetteh was at least clear-minded, and I thought that on another visit I would get her history on tape. I never made it. The stories of their lives and Elmina would disappear with them.

I returned to Accra to find my father in quite a joyous mood. It seemed my visit in itself was a healing balm. Everyone told me, behind his back of course, how happy he was that I had taken time mostly just to visit him. That evening, we visited my sister Patricia's mother-in-law and took in a Hearts of Oak versus Asante Kotoko soccer match on television. The next day, I was on my way back to North Carolina, and I checked in early in the afternoon at the airport so we could have dinner at the Landing Restaurant close to the terminal building. We had dinner outdoors because the weather was great.

Even though he seemed happy, he had a distant look in his eyes. He was dressed in an embroidered short-sleeved shirt cream in color. He sat facing the city, and I sat facing the restaurant. He seemed to be looking ahead to his time-limited future. I had no appetite; so I had a beer, and he had a pineapple juice. My good friend, Nana Asante - Sakyi, soon joined us. He always ribbed "the old man," a name he reviled, about how young he looked. He loved flattery, which confirmed his identity as an Ulzen. My maternal grandmother, Mrs. Elizabeth Andrews, always told me that my father's father was a sharp dresser complete with gold guard, walking stick, and hat. She told me this often because I was named after him and my casual ways, I believe, disturbed her more than she let on, for she was never one to utter a cross word.

We said our farewells; and after a firm handshake, for the first time since he got ill, it occurred to me that this could have been our last handshake. Suddenly I realized, as always, he was a step ahead of everyone else. Mister organization!

St. Augustine's College, Cape Coast

The author at age 8 in Kumasi, Ghana

IX

In October 1993, I had recently returned to Toronto from a year on sabbatical in the United States and was settling back into my practice and teaching activities in Toronto. My father had returned after his retirement to Ghana after twenty-six years of work in higher education and administration, which took him through Zambia, Lesotho, Botswana, and Swaziland. Later, from his headquarters in Nairobi, Kenya, he worked all over the continent of Africa, advancing the cause of literacy and adult education. This work took him to every country on the continent of Africa as he toiled to improve programs to eradicate the scourge of illiteracy, which he believed, quite rightly, was always the twin of poverty. He visited many western capitals regularly, raising funds for this war. Such was the life of one of Africa's first NGO executives. He had at this time established the first permanent secretariat for the African Adult Education Association.

One fine morning in the fall of 1993, I received a special delivery letter from Ghana. I couldn't decipher the unfamiliar writing on the envelope. The envelope revealed a scraggily handwriting, which bore a faint resemblance to my father's usual calligraphic script. I was confused for more than a moment because he always wrote with the beautiful precision of a typewriter.

The contents revealed a sick man in hospital in Accra after a series of heart attacks only six weeks after returning home to Ghana. On the flight from Toronto to Zurich, I shared a row with two guys. As it turned out, they were brothers; one had a distinctly Nordic accent, and the other one spoke with our garden-variety North American English accent. They were returning from Nova Scotia, having raced there because they thought their father was about to breathe his last. He had bounced back, surprisingly, and they were punishing the vodka without restraint as the jet purred toward Europe. I still had 37 Military Hospital in Accra on my mind, and I wondered if I'd be as lucky as these two brothers.

His heart was failing. He looked older than I ever thought he could appear. The moment I arrived, he passed me a large brown envelope. His will. He asked me to open it. I declined, not wanting to get morbid though the situation was definitely grave.

I informed my brother and two sisters in Canada and UK with a quick "sit. rep." (situation report). My youngest sister Patricia was a pharmacist at this very hospital, and at that time, a lieutenant in the Ghana Army. She had borne the burden of dealing with his fears, tantrums, anxiety, and the extended family's frustrations alone until I arrived. We decided we had to fly him out to UK for another opinion and further treatment. The cost and the fear of possible cardiac surgery horrified him. This is a man who ducked surgery when he developed appendicitis and opted for mega doses of antibiotics in 1960. He was treated at home then by a distant cousin and physician Dr. H. H. Phillips, who was later Dean of the Ghana Medical School when I was a student there.

Unknown to my father, while he was in hospital, his older sister Elizabeth had died. She had been living with their youngest sister, Mrs. Mary Folson, when my father joined the household from Nairobi since his tenant had refused to move from his home in Accra. "Big Mama" as she was affectionately known, was as extroverted and flamboyant as the Ulzens were. She was always in for the sweet nectar of life and was quite infectious with her attachment to good living. Paradoxically, this was married to the typical Ulzen love of simplicity. She had been struggling with what appeared to be cancer but died suddenly in her sister's living room from an apparent ruptured aortic aneurysm as she rose to go to bed.

It made no sense to me for my father to be informed of this tragic event immediately because of his own condition. So as he lived out his days of boredom and anxiety on the Anoff Ward, his sister's body lay in the morgue barely fifty yards away. He asked of her every evening, and I dutifully extended her greetings and best wishes to him. I restricted visitors to only members of the conspiracy of silence.

One evening, as I ended my visit with him, we were walking down the long verandah or open corridor of the hospital ward. Suddenly I heard, "I'm afraid." "Of what?" I asked evenly. "I'm just afraid," he deadpanned. It was a horribly humbling moment. The weak vitality we had mustered just dissolved into the wispy night air of Accra. This giant of our lives, this *borebore* (innovator), this visionary who, apparently without fear, set out with his three oldest children for a then unknown place called Lusaka a quarter century ago, afraid? I muttered hesitantly, without conviction, "Don't worry, everything will be all right." "How long do I have?" he shot back, keeping the pointless discussion going. I stopped walking. I looked him in his misty eye. "Dad, this can be managed and if you are lucky, ten maybe fifteen years... no one really knows."

In the end, he got seven years; said with a teacher's exactitude, he had passed the test of life and thanked each of his children for all their love and support. He was happy to have had a few years to participate again in public life in Ghana before the final bell. He was appointed to chair the board of directors of the Bureau of Ghanaian Languages two years before the end. He was full of gratitude to his country, for the trust reposed in him. He saw the appointment, small as it was, as recognition of his desire to continue to serve his country. He chose to view it as a vindication that he had been wrongly judged when he was fired from his job as Registrar of Kwame Nkrumah University of Science and Technology in Kumasi after Ghana's first coup d'état in 1966.

X

I must not have wanted to go. For the first time in my entire life, I missed my flight. My wife Ekua and I had spent the afternoon making some last minute purchases of various anticipated necessities for the funeral in Ghana. We returned to her sister, Abena's home, only to find out our flight had already departed.

"Yes, there's another flight for London leaving at 8:50 p.m., and there's room on it, but you have to show up at the counter to get on," the Canadian Airlines representative informed me at the other end of the line. There was a small matter of *banku* and fried fish waiting to be vanquished but time was simply not patient on this day. I sped down the Highway with our flotilla of bags as the *banku* and fish met their destiny in Ekua's careful hands. I was driving and my appetite could not be located. We were unfortunate to collide with a ticket agent who was lacking both in knowledge and confidence. This turned the change over to the new flight into a major production. My heart was ticking like a time bomb. I am barely patient with waiting at counters at the best of times.

After checking every little scrap of paper at the counter, we stumbled toward security and the gate. The cabin door was decisively shut seconds after we entered the aircraft. We walked to the very end of the airplane and found our seats. My head was pounding then I remembered. "Where is the money?" I said to my wife and myself at the same time. "What money?"

"The money for the funeral." I checked my pockets as the plane pulled back. The stewardess was already droning through the great attributes of the seat belt, the seat as a flotation device and how to use the oxygen masks in case the cabin pressure fell. All my bodily pressures were falling fast, and my mind was retracing every step of the day. As the plane pulled back, I stood up automatically and opened the overhead cabin on the other side of my aisle seat. In one rapid second, I searched through the outside pocket of my overnight bag. The warm crisp feel of the $100 bills greeted my fingers. I asked the puzzled stewardess for some Tylenol and a glass of water and then sank into my seat. I shut my eyes.

The house had lost its center. Red eyes welcomed us. His able and faithful "adopted" son, Ebo Quainoo, said again and again, "He deceived us." "It is death which has deceived us all," I replied carefully. "We will do whatever we have to do to send him off properly." There were so many pieces of so many lives he held together delicately, which were now adrift in a sea of increasing confusion. All the pathological behaviors of others that he had gently tolerated were now stripped naked for all to see without his patient protection and eternal optimism. His young servants and tenants were unsure of what the future held, and it looked bleak. Their guide was no more. Requests, affirmations, and promises. "Yes, yes, and yes. Okay."

My mother had arrived from her home in Takoradi the morning after he died, having been afraid to get there on time. She had always avoided funerals, but this one was right at her feet. She already had the home in her territorial and paranoid grip, seeing enemies everywhere. The house staff was uncertain of their tomorrow. Their benevolent master was no more. Their eyes to the world were permanently closed, and they looked to a new leader and further guidance. Trust was scarce as a currency of discourse at 1530 Palace Close. I busied myself with the day-to-day details of making decisions. No one was satisfied with anything. I understood that my father, friend and ever-present companion, was gone forever; and nothing short of a resurrection would satisfy us. I knew because I wished it too.

The feuds were many, big and small, important and trivial. Yet everyone claimed to be motivated by his or her love for him. Between my aunt Mary, the head of their family, and me, the dance was not graceful because the tune was composed in a hurry. The intrigues of some of his nephews and nieces left much to be desired. The attempts to belatedly change the program of events after we had received a commitment in writing were beneath comment. At this point, I was determined to go against my instincts and avoid conflict for the sake of the dead man. I am not one to back away from a confrontation, especially if it is needlessly visited upon me. It made me wonder about natural justice. Why others were alive and such a good and peace loving man gone. No rush. Everyone bargains with death and loses. He had won so many times that we were taking his hard-won victories over the dread of death for granted. Like an aged fighter, he was getting weary of climbing into the ring and at seventy-three; he finally took the full count, and it was all over.

I knew he would want all Akan traditional and Roman Catholic procedures to be followed faithfully. A small delegation made of my father's youngest sister Mary; Mr. Ghansah, an old family friend; my wife Ekua; and I made it from Auntie Mary Folson's at Tesano to Cantonments where he lived. The now undisputed head of family, His Lordship Justice Hayfron-Benjamin, my father's nephew, was expecting us. With his uncle now dead, there was no questioning his role as the head of the Nyanyiwa family. He was no more a perpetual regent for an ailing head who had spent most of his tenure overseas nonetheless. His Lordship, as he was called even at home, was everything his uncle would never have wanted to be if he had lived ten lives. His position in life seemed central to his identity. The person within was hard to find. He was opinionated and knew everything including what it was like inside a coffin, though he had not yet been introduced to death. He stammered through the *amanee*. Now we were face to face. I handed him a bottle of appropriately aged Glenffidich whisky to break the ice and as a sign of respect for his position as my father's successor at the head of the Nyanyiwa family. He was surprised, having been misinformed by his "lieutenants" to believe that I knew nothing of Akan protocol. I spoke very traditional Fanti and followed all formal protocols, which also contradicted his poorly gathered intelligence before my arrival. The judge had misjudged me greatly. By this time, I had decided that I had an administrative duty to perform as the oldest son, so I had little interest in emotion. There would be time for me to mourn later. I had cried enough already. His Lordship had to represent the maternal family, and I had to keep my brother, sisters, and mother in line until Edward Ulzen was safely returned to dust. He affectionately caressed the twenty-year-old Glenfiddich with his tremulous hand. He had to have some measure of control or we were in for a truly bleak and black week. We agreed on the day-to-day planning and endured his need for primacy over matters great and infinitesimal. He knew it all. Unlike his uncle who was authoritative but decidedly modest, he was authoritarian and well acquainted with vanity. His trembling hand shook each one offered him. "We shall meet at the morgue."

"One thirty."

XI

This was the second trip to the morgue. We had visited him for the first time yesterday. He was laid out on a gurney; his natural privacy barely protected. Here, indeed, all men were equal. This was the final destination. It mattered not whether you were a polyglot, spoke only Fanti, French, English, or Latin. Pauper or prince, on foot daily or whether you rode in a palanquin. This was the humbling end. As we say, "*Nyimpa nse hwee*" (Man is but nothing).

His face held a most comforting expression. It was that of a determined wince as he breathed his last in this existence. I muttered, mostly to myself but also to those with me, "Daddy, we are here to do our duty to you." I touched his cold, lifeless arm. His sister Mary barely let out the endearing "Brother," as he was fondly referred to by mostly his younger sisters. We were comforted by his expression of optimism and confidence even in death. Pure rigor mortis! Now, I was ready. I remembered the soldiers' handshake. He knew my optimism, though not cynical, was just a dream. He knew that was the last time. He knew it. Ekua and my cousin Araba Folson said nothing. Araba protected him till her mother and I arrived from the United States. If his body was not protected and ended up in the custody of some unfriendly maternal relative, we would be done for. It is amazing how the most educated among us can claim a dead body with more vigor than was ever exerted in a relationship of love during the person's life.

We sat in the shade, my dark glasses firmly plastered over my tired eyes. My sister Angelina punctuated our silent conversation with gently rolling tears of want of what was no more. A father's undying love for his children. The love, the earnest concern, the faith, and strength of optimism and, yes, that beautiful style.

His maternal relatives, charged with the duty of giving him his final bath, were in the medical school morgue, at work. Suddenly, I welcomed a comforting epiphany. It struck me as we waited with our eyes fixed on the entrance of the building that the Akan arrangement of the *Ebusua* or maternal family performing certain functions for the dead had some real value. After all, he was their prince. They would not entrust the delicate duty of bathing him to any stranger. His children would be too distraught to perform these duties. I began to feel less angry at the central presence of his extended family. This epiphany comforted me the rest of the way. Everyone had a job to do.

We brought him home in a small convoy of cars; the siren on the ambulance blaring senselessly as it rolled past the gates into the compound. He entered his home for the very last time. Though he had lived through his fair share of love of pomp and circumstance, this loud siren wouldn't qualify. He would have considered it one of "those stupid Ghanaian things." Tomorrow, he would go to mass and then make the journey to Elmina, his historic hometown, of which he was always so proud. He believed truly that the history of Elmina told the story of the modern world as we know it today. The stories of the "discovery" of America, the ignominious slave trade, the Ashanti-British wars, ambivalent Dutch colonialism, British imperialism, and the African independence movement all met in Elmina at different times.

We were all in a state of calm, strangely because he was back home. The professional morticians took over the business of readying him for his last social outing. Lying on a simple woven mat, on the floor of his small office addition to his modest house, he appeared to be taking a nap. He was back home, and it felt okay as long as the rest of the world didn't keep coming and calling with heartfelt condolences to remind us that this was a false and ephemeral feeling of wholeness in the family. His nap continued, and each time I came round, I thought he would ask for a glass of water or something. He lay there peacefully in his white long johns, clean-shaven, and in characteristic peace with himself and all as always.

"Who has the clothes?" the young mortician's assistant asked. "What a way to make a living." I thought quietly to myself. I produced my longtime overnight travel bag, in which resided a dark suit and other accessories required for the journey to the village. This was the first time I had ever bought a suit for my father. I bought a black suit for myself and told the salesperson I needed another one for a guy the same height but one size larger. He inquired whom it was for. "A very good friend," I answered thoughtfully and honestly. He was indeed the most faithful friend I had ever had, all my life. He was honest, reliable, and never had undeclared motives in anything we discussed or did together.

He arrived home to hysterical crying from my sister Nana, which I unfairly viewed with great suspicion. As for my mother, I had never seen her cry my whole life. She whimpered through all the expected sentiments, "Nanabanyin, my all, my everything, what am I to do now?" She had lived essentially independently of him for thirty-two years. It was only in the last ten years that they had found a comfortable rapprochement and uncharacteristic peace in their relationship. "I have forgiven him. I have forgiven them all," she said.

She went on to say, "These words were always at the tip of his tongue. He never bore anyone a grudge." Some saw it as a weakness, but we learnt over time that this was the greatest mark of courage. Nyampafo No. 7 Asafo Company was without their deliberate, kind, and compassionate leader. A prince of Elmina and the last surviving male of Angelina Akyempoma Ulzen's children had closed the door on this life.

XII

Throughout his life he had seen and experienced the best the world had to offer, but he was always discomforted by Africa's determined decline over the three-quarters of the twentieth century through which he lived. "Not in my time," he would say of Africa's promised success as a continent. "Maybe in yours," he would add, trying to keep optimism alive against an army of ugly facts to the contrary.

Two maternal female cousins of his sat in the now emptied living and dining rooms on each side of his open casket. Each time I went in, I would strike a conversation with him. He seemed really happy that it was all over. He had swallowed the bitter pill of death, and now our problems, desires, wishes and dreams were all ours. He had resigned from the daily vicissitudes of this life. He was finally a liberated man.

Periodically, arriving relatives would place gold rings on his fingers, each representing the different branches of the family who had come on this, his last night at home, to bid him farewell. The guests and well-wishers were long gone, but his two cousins, Auntie Adwoa Sekyi and Miss Mansa Mensah, sat dutifully on either side of the open casket, talking to each other and with him occasionally. They would reminisce about their shared, long-dead childhood. The old ladies seemed so young and vital in their happy memories. How he made them laugh so when they were young. "Oh, Nanabanyin…"

It was a still but clear night. The young men of the neighborhood sat in the backyard sharing their own stories of "Daddy, oh Daddy." They were listening to reggae tunes when I walked out the door from the living room across the paved outdoors, twenty paces or so to them. Like the old ladies, they were also going on and on about how he had motivated them in their struggles to better themselves. He had helped them write job-securing letters of application, and in the last months, he had embarked on a mission to teach his teenage houseboy, Okoe, to read. Each of these young men had acquired from him the habit of reading the daily papers.

I engineered a small musical coup by playing a medley of Ghanaian praise songs, which got them all singing loudly into the night. They danced, singing toward the living room where he lay under the stoic and tired eyes of his female cousins. They started an animated discussion with the dead man, reminding him of some of his more irreverent comments and admonishments of them. "*Eben mboasem nyi?*" (What sort of nonsense is this?) He had shouted once to a young man who had come to the house bare-chested in search of a friend. You had to be properly dressed to enter his compound. His bark was always supremely worse than his bite! They all laughed at how he could no longer admonish them. They then sang the medley of praise songs for him and cried at their loss, for he had been a father to all of them in different ways.

My two aunts wanted to take a break from their sentry duties, so they asked me to stay with him for a while. "Why?" I asked. There was no one else around, and I didn't see why I had to sit with him for a few minutes. They obliterated my ignorance of their duty in unison. He was their prince, and he could not be left all by himself because he was now helpless. He was to be protected every second of the way and watched over until he rested finally in the earth at the Roman Catholic cemetery in Elmina. There was nothing to debate, just new knowledge at 4:00 a.m.

The mass at Christ the King Church, right across the street from Flagstaff House, which was President Nkrumah's office when my father worked as a middle-level civil servant, brought back memories of my own early days in Accra. I attended school at Christ the King and rode in every morning with my father, who would then drive off to his office across the street after dropping me off. This was a few decades ago. It was quite a wonderful day; the sun was shining with full African determination for this, his last day on the surface of the earth. The mass was quite a celebratory affair with some tears from a few people at different times. It wasn't one of these Wailing Wall events. Most were quiet and reflective, in keeping with the man's temperament. I was too busy and vigilant to afford the luxury of tears. The officiating priest asked for the *Hallelujah* chorus to be sung, and the mass switched into full party mode. He would have loved this. The priest who delivered the homily focused on the fact that "he was a man who would not sell his principles for a bowl of porridge," referring to his disastrous firing from his job at Kwame Nkrumah University following the 1966 coup d'état, which ousted the first president. The coup d'état set in motion a nationwide witch hunt of dismissals and imprisonments of state officials and those in parastatal institutions who had even the remotest connection to the then-deposed president.

He had conveyed to us, through my sister Nana, who was in Ghana with him when he died, that he was satisfied that he had achieved God's mission for him on this earth. Such was his sense of satisfaction of a life lived. He was mostly satisfied with his success as a parent above and beyond any academic or professional achievement. I was told that from the Monday of the week in which he died, he insisted on being dressed only in white, signifying victory over death, which was surely planning to keep its appointment with him the following Friday. He was ready to cross the river to the village. He was ready for what lay beyond. On that Wednesday, he told his neighbor Mr. Brempong that he was sure this would be his last week in this life. He told all the petty traders at the Mother's Inn junction he encountered daily that he would be traveling for a while, in case they didn't see him around in the coming weeks. They probably assumed he was off to America to visit his children. He arranged all his papers; all his bills were paid, and his autobiographical notes were written. With military precision, his affairs were all in order. On Friday, he took one labored walk around his modest property and left for the hospital with my sister, her boyfriend, and one of the houseboys. He was admitted after an interminably long wait as his condition worsened. He refused the intravenous diuretic, saying he was tired and needed to rest. "It won't be long," he apparently said. Almost an hour later, in and out of delirium, he ordered his daughter out of the room. She balked. He repeated, "I say leave! I don't want you to see what is about to happen." With her back turned, he said, "My children look after each other." At 5:00 p.m., the typical end of a bureaucrat's day and week, for it was Friday; he closed shop on his life. The next generation's work began. What was our work to be?

Widowed Christiana Ulzen with Children (L – R Patricia, Thaddeus, Angelina, Edward, and Naa Ammakuma) after husband's burial service at Christ the King Church, Accra, 1999

XIII

In his retirement, there were so many things he planned to do. One of his favorite procrastinations was the origin of the Ulzen name. On my 1998 visit, he had a book on *The Dutch Archives of West Africa* and said he had a trip to make to the national archives to follow a few leads. On the genealogical pastime, his deceased older sister, "Big Mama," had done a yeoman's job of compiling the genealogy of their maternal family going back seven generations to Nana Nyanyiwa and her son Peter Vandyke, who is buried at the Dutch Cemetery in Elmina. This work was most important because among Akans, the maternal lineage is considered one's true family or *Ebusua*. Of his maternal family, which had produced many national notables including jurists, academics, physicians, diplomats, educators, craftsmen, and traders, he was always proud. He remembered his maternal grandmother, Maame Amakuma, as a wealthy woman who sponsored the education of many of her grandchildren. His mother, Angelina Aikins, Maame Amakuma's youngest child, had died in her fifties and had clearly been extremely fond of him. Her death was a real blow, and his success in life was always muted by the fact that she did not live long enough to see how he had turned out in the end. His grandfather, R. R. Aikins, came up in an interesting anecdote repeatedly over the years. He apparently enjoyed the roughhousing of his grandsons and grandnephews. He would urge them on as they boxed each other, shouting from my father's corner, "Nana, fight back harder. Move, move; use your left..." and utterances to that effect. My father was quite surprised years later to learn that the old man was blind all the time he was acting as his boxing coach!

The Nyanyiwa Nsona family, like many others in Elmina, is of both African and Dutch origins. My grandfather's second child, "Big Mama" or Mrs. Elizabeth Adjaye as she was generally known, had traced the maternal bloodlines to Ako Sika, the last known matriarch of the royal clan of *Akodaa Turo Mu*-Niezer's Garden. She was the mother of Nana Nyanyiwa and grandmother of Adwoa Esuon, Nana Sema and Kodwo Aaba (Peter Vandyke) whose grave at the Dutch Cemetery notes his death as occurring on October 14, 1882. Big Mama completed her genogram of their family on June 4, 1984. I found this information quite illuminating in understanding different personalities in my father's maternal extended family. My father had done a good job of bringing me into contact with many relatives of his from an early age. As it turned out, he understood that I would have to contend with them at the end of his life.

On the Ulzen side, not much information had been collected, as this was his paternal family and was of less importance in the Akan world. In my generation, the strict focus on the maternal lineage is more theoretical and symbolic, only becoming important at funerals when some maternal families choose to remind the bereaved children of how much power maternal relatives used to have in the rapidly vanishing past. In the present, most people bequeath their estates to their children rather than their maternal nephews, as strict tradition would dictate. Elmina is unusual in another respect. The society is matrilineal but the chieftaincy is patrilineal, as it is among Western royalty. It stands alone as the only Akan state with a patrilineal chieftaincy. An additional twist is that the successor to the chief must have been born while he was in office. This child is known as an *Apakanmuba*, a child of the palanquin.

XIV

In the fall of 1998, a few months after my most enjoyable visit to Ghana, I entered the inbox of my e-mail and noticed an e-mail from a Daniel Ulzen. I knew no one with this name, so I hesitated somewhat before the enlightening click of the mouse, wondering who on earth Daniel Ulzen is. The African mind asked, "Is this some unknown sibling?" In Africa, it is not unusual for children of a deceased man to discover each other at their father's funeral.

There was little to be concerned about for I strongly doubted my father would pull something like this on us. Daniel, as it turned out, was a German teacher and magician who believed that there were only seven Ulzens in Germany and, therefore, in the world. He had been on his own search and found my name along with my brother's on an Internet search. He was surprised to find that other Ulzens existed and was about to find out that the guy on the other end of the World Wide Web was a very black Ulzen from Africa no less!

Like many Westerners, he had no awareness of the wanderings of European men who were busy trading in Africa and siring children with dark, beautiful, and mysterious women on the proverbial Dark Continent. I informed him of the Brandenburgers who traded briefly in Ghana in the 1700s. I was convinced though that my name was Dutch in origin like most European names in Elmina. I should not have been so sure since the trading companies sometimes employed officers from other European countries. Anyhow, Daniel and I exchanged genealogical files to see if any plausible links existed. He sent me data going back into the 1700s. I sent him the names of all the Ulzens I knew as far back as my great-grandfather, Jacob A. F. Ulzen who was born in 1845. We found only a few shared names between the data sets. I also shared my anxiety about opening my e-mail with "Mzee" Ulzen who was highly amused.

Daniel Ulzen and I were both at dead ends in different countries and almost a century apart in our data. He was aware of only five Ulzens in Germany, some Ulzenhiemers and an Ulzen-Mile as well as a Herman Ulzen. He thought there were possibly some Ulzens in the Netherlands but could not be certain.

My knowledge of my family name was restricted to Ghana. I knew that Jacob, my great-grandfather had lived and worked in Calabar, Nigeria, as a colonial civil servant under the British. My old roommate at the University of Ghana, Dr. S. O. Odesola, who was a Nigerian in Ghana for the first time in his life, told me that as unusual as my surname was, he was familiar with it in the Port Harcourt area of Nigeria. We joked frequently that Jacob Ulzen must have been busy at his post in Nigeria.

In Ghana, apart from my own immediate extended family of Ulzens in Elmina, my father's two half-brothers, Patrick M. Ulzen Jr. from Sefwi-Wiawso and Issac Ulzen of Sekondi. I had heard of a lawyer from Axim and that was about it. In Sekondi, there were a lot of Ulzens including one popular soccer referee, William Frederick Ulzen. I always assumed they were descendants of my grandfather's brothers, but my dad informed me in 1998 that this was an erroneous theory.

Daniel Ulzen had a theory on the possible origin of the name and its geographic reach as far as he knew. He shared with me the theory that it was originally Scandinavian, probably Ulson or Olsen, which became more Germanic with the southern migration to Holland and Germany. He noted that the myth in his family, supported by some historical evidence, was that an earlier Ulzen had worked in the court of a German king, where it was transformed to the Germanic version we shared between Germany, the Netherlands, and Ghana. A royal angle to a name never hurts its reputation.

My dad and I tried to reconcile ourselves to this new German angle, but there was no story to tie the German, Dutch, and African Ulzens.

We were sitting yet under another clear African sky, deep into the night. I was in Accra, attending to probate issues and the like. Ebo Quainoo, one of the young men who lived in my father's compound, an adopted son as it were, continued to marvel at how many people seemed to know Daddy. He gave me a rundown of notables who came to visit, and the number of times he was sent for because some visiting delegation or government official from some country was in Ghana and had asked of him. Ebo was still astonished at how unaffected my father was by his own celebrity.

As an example, he mentioned that just a few weeks before he died, a certain European woman, apparently a professor, had gone to Elmina asking of him and had been given directions to the house at Kaneshie. She had a brief conversation with him as he was unwell and on his way to a doctor's appointment. He had given her some papers with which she left, but he never shed any light on the visit or commented on it before he died two weeks later. I asked, "Is that all?" "Yes, she left and to this day, I don't know what they talked about. So many people visit him. Sometimes, he tells us who they are; at other times, he says nothing."

My good friend Edwin Omaboe and I were the last to leave the graveside. As we walked from the Catholic cemetery to Hollywood Hotel, where the guests were being feted, I wondered who this professor could have been. My father and I spoke almost daily as his illness worsened, but he never mentioned this. I wondered just the same.

XV

My wife Ekua and I returned from the mixed emotions of Ghana. It is always affirming to re-experience the familiarity of the native soil with its peculiar heaviness, brightness, and of course, pungent smells, stagnant pools, open gutters, mosquitoes, and all that makes life a challenge. It is such a breeding ground for resilience. The air seemed so much more in tune with one's living soul.

Consumed either by guilt of not recognizing how little time we have on this earth or out of a sense of duty to complete an untold and waiting story, I began to search more fervently for anything Ulzen. I renewed my vows of marriage to the personal computer and surfed all the byways of the Internet and cyberland, knocking on the doors of any database promising to hand over knowledge pertinent to my soul's quest. My daughter Adwoa was conscripted and shared in the thrill of the hunt. I would call her to examine evidence as it downloaded into my study.

Within a few days, we came upon a Hermanus Ulzen, married to a Jacoba van Mensburg in the genealogy of Clerck. There was a scattering of members of this Dutch family related to this Van Mensburg who fought in wars in Guinea in the 1600s. This made it somewhat exciting, giving us a sense of being close to something important. The name Hermanus was the only name beyond my great-grandfather Jacob's generation that I was aware of from my conversations with my father. However, it seemed to be nowhere.

We were roaming through Enkuizen and Zeeland chambers of commerce and other items or links on the Internet related to these names.

I began to scan the book *Dutch Archives of West Africa*, which I had found open on my father's desk in his bedroom when I returned for his funeral. He had marked a few items, possibly intent on writing to the Dutch Archives or have me do so for the information of interest. The book lay with a small bound briefcase, which contained information liberated from his father's Bible years ago. The path lay on the desk, yielding no specific destination.

I was now gripped by the desire to unlock whatever Holland had to give surrounding this name. I knew at home, they laughed secretly and politely about this obsession; and my wife, it seemed, thought it was a strange twist to the mourning process. After all, one of the things we shared, my father and I, was this name; and in keeping and understanding it, our relationship would endure for all time. Everything else was dynamic and alive, and with a big part of the name dead, the breathing of new life into the name to keep it going seemed in order.

He had tried to pursue the search from the ground up. It was strange, but at his age, he was still involved in finding out after whom he was named. There was no Edward in the past. He shared Abraham as a middle name with his older brother and his grandfather. My father was known at home as Nanabanyin after a male forebear, before his father's time. The voice of history told him he was named after two people, his grandfather and someone else. The old woman who held the key to this mystery died with her knowledge. Before she departed though, she shared her reluctance to discuss his hunch about his great-grandfather. He never understood why. It is always like that. You wake up to your story with too little time left, surrounded by relatives with vanishing memories now filled with colorful confabulations. Could the other person have been his grandfather's father? Patrick Manus, my grandfather, shared the name Hermanus with his older brother Eliyah Herm Ulzen who died in infancy in 1877.

XVI

As the first born in my family, I was named after my grandfather Patrick Manus, so I reasoned that Eliyah Herm must have been named after Hermanus. Is this the Manus my father believed or was told worked as an administrator of some sort in the castle? I perused the *Dutch and Belgian Archives of West Africa*, looking for clues. I located the Dutch archives in cyberspace and sent them a list of documents, which I thought would help in my search. They wrote back saying the reference numbers were incorrect and gave me a quote of forty-two guilders to conduct the search once we resolved the classification questions. I sent them my source and waited for a response.

Within two weeks, I received an e-mail from the Netherlands, but it was not from the Dutch archives. A Dr. Van Kessel had been researching the story of the African soldiers, who had been recruited in the nineteenth century from what is now Ghana, to fight for the Dutch East Indies Army (KNIL) in Java. She had a number of names of these soldiers and had visited Elmina with the names, seeking possible descendants. One of the names in hand was a Bart Ulzen. After a few false starts in Elmina, which she had visited as a side trip while attending a conference in Accra, she was led to the Ulzen house. At the house in Sybil, Elmina, she met my older cousin Johanna Fynn-Aggrey who directed her to her uncle, Edward Ulzen in

Accra. She told the visitor, "He is the one who holds the history, collects information about it, and talks about it."

The directions were accurate, for she found the house in Kaneshie with no difficulty. She met Daddy while he was on his way to a doctor's appointment, his failing heart committing him to a polygamous marriage with all his physicians. He did not recognize the name Bart as a relative. The Java story did not resonate with him. He did not think it was related to his family. He, however, gave the good professor his son's e-mail address and asked her to check with him because he shared the interest in the origin of the Ulzen name and may have other information. Dr. Van Kessel revealed that Bart Ulzen was described in the Catholic Church's records as a "pensioned Java soldier." He was the curator of a Catholic church and also a godfather to many baptized Catholic children in Elmina in the late 1800s. I had never heard of Bart Ulzen myself, but his strong Catholic connection was a positive sign. The Ulzens are known in Elmina as staunch Catholics. From my father's generation down, the Ulzens of Sybil, Elmina, are also known as educators or academics. In the church, they are often involved as musicians. Dr. Van Kessel was told when she was directed to the Ulzen house in Elmina that "they are all teachers!"

I informed Dr. Van Kessel that I did not know of Bart but believed that his involvement with the Catholic Church made him a potential ancestor. I, however, offered the name Manus or Hermanus to her and asked if she could find anything about him, thinking that he may have been a Dutch or Euro-African official at the castle. We placed his birth date early in the nineteenth century as his putative son Jacob A. F. Ulzen was born in 1845 according to the family records. In a few short weeks, I received an e-mail from Dr. Van Kessel saying she had found a Manus Ulzen who had enlisted in the Royal Netherlands East Indies Army in 1832. He was one of the first forty-four recruits to sail to Batavia (Jakarta). She wondered if our surname was adopted because many recruits were given Dutch names on joining the army. For many reasons, I thought it unlikely that the name was adopted.

The sudden gust of new information energized my daughter Adwoa and me as we wondered where this would lead. In order to confirm if this Manus was a direct relative, I expected to find that his father was called

Jacob, following the same logic I had used to locate him in the genealogical scheme. This was not to be. The information yielded a completely different name not repeated in the more modern generations of Ulzens. He enlisted at age twenty in 1832, and he listed his father as a Roelof Ulzen; his mother was listed as Abbenada Atta, a very African woman indeed who must have been a twin, whose twin sibling may have arrived on a different day. There were many errors in transcribing African names. Her name more logically would have been Abenaba Atta, meaning the daughter of Abena, who is a twin. These records established that he was a *tapoeyer* or mulatto, and it is unlikely that he was given this name for the purposes of enlistment.

Suddenly, my memory of the commemorative Java tablet at the entrance of St. George's castle in Elmina was awakened. The hill across from the Elmina Castle, covering the north and east, was Java Hill; but I had never had a conversation with anyone who had actually identified anyone or the family as being connected to the military experience in Java. My mind traveled to all its Java associations. There were also the extensive Java wax prints—the fabric which formed the basis of most traditional clothing outside of the traditional *kente* cloth or *adinkra*, which are traditionally handwoven or hand stamped respectively—with their roots in the Ashanti.

When we lived in Lusaka, Zambia, our next-door neighbor in Olympia Park was a Dr. Van Velsen who was Dutch, as far as I knew, until he made it known one day that he was from Java. He and my father had conversations about Java, but I paid little attention to this. Van Velsen is an example of a person referred to in the Netherlands as an "Indo" or and Indo-European.

Man modeling uniform of African KNIL soldiers at Elmina – Java Museum (2003)

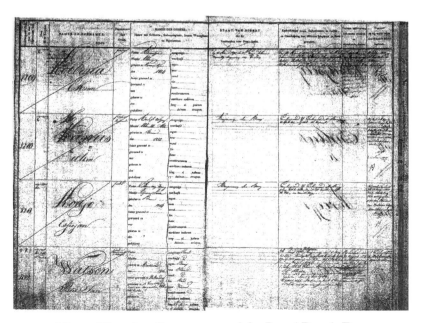

Manus Ulzen's enlistment record for Royal Dutch East Indies Army (KNIL) in 1832 – 2nd from top

XVII

The enlistment of Africans for Java was part of a complex series of events whose origins as usual lay far away from the African continent. As I understand it, at that time, the Dutch had an army that was heavily dependent on Belgians for recruitment. The Belgians, having become independent of Dutch control, were no longer a real source of recruits for the military; so the Dutch had to consider other options.

The Dutch experience in West Africa had been less profitable than expected after a presence of about two hundred years. Elmina was the headquarters of Dutch Guinea and also the only secure access to the coast for the powerful Ashanti kingdom. The Dutch, Elminians, and the Ashanti were considered allies in a region fraught with increasing conflict: a risky trade in slaves and a gold trade, which never met the expectations of the Dutch. The Dutch were always ambivalently involved with and never quite exerted themselves as a colonial power over the Africans. Britain was on its ascendancy as the most powerful naval nation in the world at the time and was increasing its activity on the coast with a view to consolidating its assets and establishing a colony. The Dutch viewed their possessions in Asia as being more economically viable and were determined to suppress the Muslim insurgency in Aceh to secure a profitable colony in modern-day Indonesia.

In 1830, two events, Belgian independence and the Java War forced the

Dutch to examine recruitment possibilities in West Africa more seriously. They had naively thought that competitive conditions of service offered would attract young men to a military career in the East Indies. Various relationships of servitude existed on the coast and in the interior exclusive of the transatlantic slave trade. These relationships and the abolition of slavery made this recruitment effort a subject of suspicion both from other European powers on the coast and the local aristocracies. Domestic servitude, pawnshop, and "owned tradesmen" were common locally. These members of the servant class were usually highly integrated into the extended family network of their owners and were unlikely to leave Elmina for the East Indies.

An experimental effort to recruit one hundred fifty Africans toward an eventual African Corps in Java began in 1831, but the Dutch soon discovered that there was little enthusiasm from the locals.

An eventual African Corps in Java began in 1831 but the Dutch soon discovered that there was little enthusiasm from the locals. Governor Frans Last expressed his concerns thus: "Immigrants, even temporary migrants are completely unknown and strange to the Negroes of this coast from Cape Apollonia in the west of Elmina to Popo to the east. No one thinks of leaving the country of their birth".

A debate continued in Dutch government and military circles on the merits and demerits of recruiting tapoeyers (Africans of Dutch ancestry) as opposed to "children of nature," Africans from the interior who were presumed to be more submissive. Tapoeyers were believed less likely to accept abuses, but on the other hand, they were likely to understand European military discipline. An inducement of ten to twelve florins was offered to interest the prospects along with a *delegatien* or advance, which could be paid to relatives or creditors back home. It appears that the commonest motives for young men to undertake this experience would be indebtedness, plain lack of opportunity, or simply an interest in adventure.

At age twenty, Manus Ulzen, a *tapoeyer*, was one of the first forty-four to sail to the Netherlands East Indies on the *Clara Henrietta*. He sailed on March 14, 1832, as the only corporal among the seven African recruits who joined the Europeans on board that ship. The journey took about 120 days from the Netherlands to Batavia (Jakarta), Indonesia. The conditions of service were a minimum of six years followed by a choice of repatriation to Elmina or the renewal of the contract for a further six years. Injured men qualified for a pension just as those who completed their contract. The pay for privates, corporals, and sergeants was twenty-one cents, twenty-nine cents, and thirty-seven cents per day respectively plus food. On enlistment, they each received a piece of cloth or four gallons of rum, clothing, and a hammock. Corporals were usually soldiers who had already been in Dutch service, and the rank of sergeant was achieved only after active service in Java. Manus Ulzen apparently demanded to be made a corporal as a requirement for recruitment because he had visited or lived in Europe previously and spoke some Dutch, offering to act as a translator. He was successful in entering the service of the Royal Dutch East Indies Army (KNIL) at the rank of corporal. He had no prior army experience, and the six men on his ship did not warrant a corporal rank. Of the seven African recruits who boarded the *Clara Henrietta,* Ulzen would be the only one to return to the land of his birth. Four of his companions died while in KNIL service, one settled in Java, and one ended up in a mental institution in Batavia.

He disembarked in Batavia (Jakarta) on June 1, 1832. He was wounded by the enemy at Lampong, South Sumatra, on January 14, 1835, apparently having been shot in the left thigh during the military campaign. He was discharged as a result of his injuries, and when asked where he would like to enjoy his pension, he replied, "I want to stay here with my comrades, and if ever some of them will return to Guinea, then I will join them". He was formally discharged from the army by decree on July 25, 1835. As a result of this, he left the Indies for Holland on August 27, 1835. He sailed on the ship *Schoon Verbond* with seven other returning soldiers. They sailed via the Cape of Good Hope and sailed past Elmina to Texel, an island at the northern tip of the Netherlands. They arrived in mid-winter on December 4, 1835. Manus continued on his subsequent trip on a much smaller boat from Texel over the Zuiderzee to Harderwijk, the home base of the colonial troops, where he was provided with winter clothing. On December 11, 1835, the commander of the colonial garrison reported to the department of colonies on the arrival of a detachment of returning soldiers from the East Indies with the *Schoon Verbond*. One of these soldiers was an African corporal with documents stating that he was entitled to an annual pension of f 142, payable in Elmina, Africa. As a result of his war injuries, the corporal walked on two crutches.

On January 10, 1836, Colonel De Muralt dispatched him to the military hospital in Utrecht with "an excellent and comfortable covered carriage" and accompanied by a responsible person for further treatment of his leg injury. Apparently, the wound had developed complications. Some weeks later, the hospital reported that the leg probably had to be amputated. It is unclear if it ever was. Manus Ulzen indicated to a senior officer who visited patients at the military hospital that he had been promised a bronze medal because of the wounds he had sustained in battle. He claimed to have given the document attesting to this to an official on arrival at Harderwijk. The authorities found this irregular since such medals were awarded only after twelve years of service. Manus insisted that this promise had been made to him, so in the end, King Willem I approved the exception and proposed that the medal be given to him on board the ship on his way to Elmina. This was presumably to prevent setting a precedent and a flood of similar requests. This new exception later became the rule for African veterans to stimulate further recruitment in Elmina. He also received the twelve guilders, which came with the award.

On January 19, 1837, *De Jonge Adriana* sailed from the small port of Hellevoetsluis. On board the ship, Ulzen received the bronze medal awarded to him by King Willem I for his service in the East Indies with the accompanying ribbon and certificate plus the premium of twelve guilders. Among the correspondence given to the ship's captain for Gov. Tonnebjer in Elmina was a letter concerning Manus Ulzen. It stated that he was to receive a lifelong pension of f142 florins per annum to be paid in monthly installments or other terms at the discretion of the governor. The first installment was to be paid on March 1, 1837. The minister advised the governor to treat "the said M. Ulzen in such a way as will be conducive to the encouragement of other Negroes to enter into our service".

By way of comparison, retired sergeant-major Heindrik Ulzen, possibly a brother or cousin of Manus, received a pension of only 108 guilders a year after an army career of more than twenty-five years with the permanent force of St. George d'Elmina. The trip to Java was apparently worth a few extra guilders if you came out of the experience with your life. Manus Ulzen arrived home in Elmina on March 19, 1837, a day after the signing of the treaty between the Dutch King and the Ashanti King Kwaku Dua I to secure two thousand men for military service in the East Indies.

The ship on which Manus returned, the *De Jonge Adriana* left for Java on March 26, with eighty new recruits on board. On April 1, 1837, Manus Ulzen must have witnessed the return to Elmina of General Verveer and his retinue from Kumasi, no doubt surrounded with much pomp, pageantry, and circumstance. This group included two young Ashanti princes, Kwasi Boakye and Kwame Poku, destined for a Dutch education in Europe as part of the accord between the Dutch and the Ashanti.

Prince Diponegoro, Javanese Prince who led the insurgency against the Dutch during the Java War (1825 -1830); with permission from Museum Bronbeek, Arnhem

Portrait of Kwasi Boakye (1847) one of two Ashanti Princes sent to the Netherlands for a Dutch education by his uncle King Kwaku Dua I of Ashanti in in 1837.

King Willem I

King Willem I

XVIII

Manus was a young man of twenty-five when he returned to Elmina. It is unclear how he spent his time. He was however allotted some land on Java Hill and in 1846 along with some other *tapoeyers,* built his house, and settled on the hill for the rest of his life. It appears that his return, along with others to Elmina, was played up by the Dutch to buttress their claim that the military experience in Indonesia was not a disguised form of slavery. In heated correspondence between the Dutch and British in 1840, the Dutch stated,

> "… It indicates that men already returned from the Island of Java with a pension and again dwelling on the coast of Guinea; and it will not be useless to add, that one of the Africans enlisted is at present time promoted to the rank of officer…"

The Dutch had faced increasing criticism that many of the recruits had little choice. This was true for a majority of the native recruits who were brought from Kumasi. They were essentially slaves whose masters sought payment for the enlistment of their servants into the army. Most veterans did not come from Elmina and could not truly return to their native home, having been sold into the service from points north of Kumasi prior to their release from bondage into a new servitude in the Dutch military. After completing their contracts, most veterans therefore stayed in Java, founding a number of Afro-Indonesian towns like Semarang, Purowerajo, and Solo. Their sons tended to continue in the military tradition in the East Indies.

The recruitment process under Governor Lans, who succeeded Governor Last, was highly corrupt and with the collusion of the *Asantehene* (king of Ashanti) and some of the coastal chiefs, payments of the *delegatien* were withheld from the pay of the recruits at embarkation and misappropriated. When Manus Ulzen signed up, he took a three-month pay advance presumably paid to his mother Abbenaba Atta. He continued to send money to her during his years of service.

Even Governor Last noted, "Free Negroes will never encourage their slaves to enlist because they regard them [the slaves] as consisting a part of their family." He informed The Hague that the recruitment had largely become a matter of obtaining slaves from Ashanti in collusion with their masters. He doubled the minimum term of enlistment to twelve years and offered one ounce of gold dust as a sign-on bonus, which went to the masters of the recruit. By 1836, Governor Lans had exceeded the recruitment target through these corrupt methods with open knowledge of The Hague.

The African soldiers had been a military success in Java, and the pressure to recruit more of them continued to rise. They were placed on equal terms with the Europeans, above the Indonesian native. Emboldened by these successes, the Dutch mounted a major diplomatic mission to recruit two thousand soldiers from the kingdom of Ashanti in 1836.

Major General Jan Verveer led this embassy to Ashanti. He found that almost all his recruits were in reality slaves. He, however, tried to circumvent this ethical dilemma if they willingly wished to enter Dutch military service. How much free will could a slave in Kumasi really have? If after being freed they were unwilling to enlist, they were released to their master or were free to leave. The king of Ashanti was offered six thousand guns, two thousand pounds of gunpowder and other gifts in exchange for the promise of two thousand men. Verveer also started a practice of an elaborate embarkation ritual in Elmina involving cannons being fired in honor of their enlisted men. The embarkation for the East Indies took place in a "ceremonial and impressive fashion." He also issued certificates of manumission to the men, having individually been interviewed of their intent to enlist of their own free will. Each was paid two and a half ounces of gold and the *delegatien* was cancelled. As a result of Verveer's efforts, 2,100 men were transported to Indonesia between December 1836 and February 1842.

Life in Java was far from idyllic as mutinies and numerous revolts occurred because of racism experienced by the soldiers over time. They were described as being "Life in Java was far from idyllic, as mutinies and numerous revolts occur." They were after all, free men. In the 1850s, the Dutch continued to recruit, having a mulatto agent, Pieter de Heer, in Kumasi to facilitate this. He was under strict instructions to seek free men and had to increase the sign-on bonus to facilitate this. The pressure of a continued demand for troops from the East Indies guided policy as the British kept a watchful eye on the process. Between 1855 and 1872, another 796 men were transported to the East Indies.

From the *Rotterdams Walvern* in 1832 to the *Robertus Hendrikus* in 1872, a total of 3,080 Africans sailed as soldiers of the KNIL from Elmina to the Netherlands East Indies. Each of these men was fighting to free himself from something. Some were liberating themselves from debt, and others from bondage. They fought for the Netherlands in the colonial wars against other oppressed people yet to find the door of freedom. Such was the irony of the Black Dutchmen of Java. Many paid the ultimate price for their quest to be free. Was Manus Ulzen a young adventurer, heavily indebted at age twenty, or simply a man without skills to try anything else? All his male ancestors had served the Dutch in some capacity, but none appeared to have had much formal education. Formal education for Africans was virtually nonexistent, but some mulattoes received education in a small school in conjunction with Christian evangelical efforts of the Dutch.

It is likely that Manus Ulzen was an illiterate because many *tapoeyers* were left uneducated like other local children. In 1817 De Marée wrote that children of European fathers on the Gold Coast were not being brought up any better than indigenous ones. Rev. Beckeringh observed in 1756 that in Elmina one often saw "many children of white fathers wandering amid the heathen."

An 18th Century Dutch Ship

African Street (Gang Afrikan II) in Kampung Afrikan (Afrikan Village), in Purworejo Regency, Central Java where Indo –Africans settled.

African Street (Gang Afrikan II) in Kampung Afrikan (Afrikan Village), in Purworejo Regency, Central Java where Indo –Africans settled.

Jan Kooi – The most decorated African Soldier in Java; he served from 1869 – 1888. Reproduced with permission, Bronbeek Museum, Arnhem

XIX

At the beginning of the new millennium, a year later, only three out of the five children were back in Ghana to unveil the grave and headstone of Daddy (as we always called him). I was back at the house on Palace Close, Kaneshie. Every morning at about 11:00 a.m., I hydrated myself with a cold Star beer and continued the process of going through his papers. We found them largely organized in a logical fashion. No surprise there. Each period, each job, each country was properly categorized.

Apart from programs for many adult education conferences he attended or organized, his personal papers revealed his lifelong preoccupations. His investment in having his name cleared of any suggested wrongdoing at KNUST was preeminent. In numerous letters to different Ghanaian heads of state, he sought to have any official records suggesting he had done wrong expunged. He had never been charged with any offense, yet indirectly, he was marked as a persona non grata for many years, especially during the period in which the military junta ruled and their puppet civilian regime which had followed. Numerous UN jobs were denied him on account of the refusal of the Ghanaian authorities to provide the necessary approval for support after he had been chosen. He eventually won limited approval to work as consultant in numerous UN projects in his field.

He was also concerned about how his youngest daughter, my sister Patricia, would fare after his death. He needn't have worried. This was not an issue that occupied him much in later years as Pat was considered by all of us very much our sister. As the eldest, I was committed to this unity because as a child, she had no choice in how she arrived at the doorstep of life. He was gladdened and comforted by my views on this issue. I insisted that she be treated no differently from anyone else. He kept many, too many, funeral announcements and biographies of departed friends, colleagues, and others. He wondered, I suppose what the program of his final event would look like. His numerous battles with various organizations and agencies on contractual matters and issues of principle were kept. He was always preoccupied with the written record as evidence of the truth in any given situation.

There was some unlikely correspondence from his nephew Kwamena, who had lived in his home for four years rent-free. This revolved around his mother's wonderful genealogical work. For some strange reason, his nephew felt Daddy was laying claim to his mother's work. His older sister, Mrs. Elizabeth Adjaye (Big Mama) had completed her extensive genealogy of their *Ebusua* (maternal extended family) in 1984. Big Mama and Daddy had some differences in opinion about the accuracy of parts of the document on the grounds that some non-blood relations might have been included as family members; and he sought, as usual, to set the record straight. He had discussed possible revisions with his older sister, the author of this work. It seems that this son of hers, and possibly other children, seemed to take this honest difference in opinion very personally. The Akans have a saying, "Your nephew is your enemy." Meaning, because your maternal nephews are your heirs, they may plot to succeed you before their time.

The most intriguing finding for me was father's enrollment at the Middle Temple, London, UK, as an external student to study law while he was registrar for special duties at the National University of Lesotho. He had completed about 50 percent of the program in 1979, when he accepted the position of executive secretary of the African Adult Education Association in Nairobi. He then abandoned this program as he became quite busy with travel, fundraising, writing, and other job-related pursuits. He was a distance educator, and true to his belief in lifelong education, he had planned to qualify as a lawyer as an extramural student. He never discussed this with any of us. The process of going through his papers brought the three of us, Angelina, Patricia, and me, laughter, tears, and sober reflection on the meaning of life. Angelina was particularly effusive about the simplicity at the core of such a fulfilling life. Patricia and I split the cold Star beers, and Angelina did most of the reflection on the somber aspects of life.

XX

We arrived in Elmina on Saturday, October 21, for the memorial mass scheduled for the next day. The priest would come and unveil the tomb and then we would proceed to mass atop Saint Joseph's Hill. We would then return to the Ulzen house for a small family gathering. I had been to the cemetery earlier to be sure all the words on the grave were correctly spelt. Not that much could be done to correct any possible errors. In any event, I needn't have worried. My uncle, Anthony Clement, master of precision, had taken great care to ensure that all was well. He had applied his engineer's expertise to this project and had done so with dedication to the man who had effectively been his father throughout his life. Mr. Clement or Uncle Ebow, as he is generally known, is one of my mother's younger brothers and had lived under my parents' tutelage since he was fourteen years old. He insisted on paying for our father's coffin, and we all understood why it had to be so. All the Latin and English words were as they should have been.

As we sat downstairs in the living room of P. M. Ulzen's house, we discussed the plans and shared our thoughts and feelings on the genealogical revelations of the past year. As we talked, the Spartan nature of our surroundings struck me. It reminded me of how simply my father kept our furnishings and surroundings throughout his life. On the ride from Accra to Elmina, Angelina and I went through fifty or so pages of family genealogy sent to me by Dr. Michel Doortmont, an expert in the history of

Euro-African families in West Africa. Dr. Doortmont and I had failed to meet on my trip to the Netherlands in the previous year where I attended the tenth biannual reunion of the Belanda Hitam (Black Dutchmen) as a guest of honor. We had chatted on the phone as he had been unwell.

We entertained ourselves with the strange names like Moselit, Rodolfus, and Swait Ulzen. We were also sobered and saddened that the plethora of information had arrived within less than a year after the death of our father, Edward, who had an abiding interest in searching for this information. He always sought knowledge if it could possibly be found, but his failing health in his last years had prevented him from pursuing this. Angel was most personally hurt by this, even though she felt strongly that it was indeed "the right time to die."

As my youngest surviving paternal aunt Mary leafed through the pages of the Doortmont data, she discovered that her name, Ekua Esuon, was that of the wife of Hermanus Ulzen of Java. For the first time in her life, she now understood that she was named after her father's paternal grandmother. She explained that in their time, they grew up rather traditionally and were close only to their maternal relatives. She hardly knew any of her father's relatives. Other Ulzens were merely a distant curiosity. She regretted that she never met Georgius Rodolfus Ulzen who lived in Elmina and died only in 1965. Many different aspects of this information came up, but the biggest surprise of all was the fact that their great grandfather Hermanus Ulzen had been a Java veteran. His son, Bart, younger brother to their grandfather Jacob A. F. Ulzen was described as a "pensioned Java soldier" in the history of the Catholic church in Elmina. This appears to have been an error, for there is no evidence that he ever went to Java. Manus Ulzen served as the first church keeper of the Catholic Church in Elmina in its *status nascendi*.

The matrilineal obsession in our society had led to a real paucity of interest and knowledge of these patrilineal relatives and their simple, rich, and adventurous lives. The Doortmont document included the will of Hermanus Ulzen, clearly identifying his four sons Jacob, Henry, Bart, and N. Ulzen. We all imagined how happy Daddy would have been to know this before his passing. I opined that after his meeting with Dr. Ineke van Kessel, it was clear to him that the answer would soon be in our hands. That much he knew. The visit must have been the most treasured gift he ever received. I said, "He saw Canaan but…" Another round of cold beer! Dr. Van Kessel and Mr. and Mrs. Cordus arrived at the Ulzen house in Sybil, just as I was wondering how I would contact them. Ineke had, of course, been to this house before and knew just how to find us.

The Corduses were an interesting couple in their appearance. Most Elminians on the street would describe them as white (*abrofo*) even though their features were mainly Asiatic and African. They looked like an Asian version of the modern-day mixed and remixed Elmina mulatto. We continued our journey into history as their visit brought the Java story to life on the main floor of the P. M. Ulzen home. They were both descendants of African Java veterans who had settled in Indonesia. They had previously asked me what they would need to wear for the next day's activities, and I assured them that as long as they had drinks, "Every faux pas would be overlooked." There is no problem in Akan society which cannot be resolved with or dissolved in alcohol, especially with schnapps from the Netherlands.

It was a day as bright as any other was. It was not terribly hot thankfully. Dr. Van Kessel dressed in her blue-and-white trademark African shirt and the Corduses rather casually clad were seated and joined the circle as we continued our conversations about history. They were guided in greeting those already seated from right to left or in a counter-clockwise fashion as Akan custom dictates and then took their seats. The circle of conversation occupied the western half of the room as those on the eastern half of the room engaged in gustatory ventures, drinking, and carrying on other discussions of the present epoch. I, of course, had suddenly become the *Okyeame* or spokesperson for the visitors, for I carried their story. I stood up and asked for permission to address the small but expectant gathering. I addressed the head of family, His Lordship Justice Hayfron-Benjamin, who had succeeded my father in the position as head of the Nyanyiwa family of Elmina. My father had never truly occupied the position as he had been away for so many years. I am told, though, that in the few years that he managed the affairs of the family before his demise, he ushered in a period of peace and order. I believe that this unusual situation made for a strange relationship between this man and my father, his uncle. My father was certainly a more accepting and less authoritarian figure in contrast to his nephew who, in my opinion, could not wait to fully take charge of the family of which he had been in control of quite frankly for decades.

I began by recognizing that we were meeting in the house of the late Patrick Manus Ulzen who was the grandson of Hermanus Ulzen, who had brought Dr. Van Kessel's search and our search into unity.

There was some humor about my contradictory position as the eldest son of the man whose passing we were commemorating and my immediate role as spokesman for the Dutch visitors. The gathering was as simple as my father would have wanted it. It was a small family affair in his father's home. In Akan protocol, a great deal of improvisation is allowed as long as one explains himself and seeks permission. Improvisation is the only consistent feature of Akan discourse. American jazz music owes a great debt to Akans. Having made my predicament quite clear, the story of my visit as a guest of honor to the tenth annual meeting of the Black Dutchmen (Belanda Hitam) in the Netherlands was unfolded.

Daan Cordus (Left) and his wife Eef Cordus – Klink (Right)
elders of Belanda Hitam community in the Netherlands.
Daan and grandson Wouter Neuhaus (Middle).

Author with his mother Mrs. Christiana Ulzen, his brother
Edward and sister Dr. Angelina Ulzen – Chela on St. Joseph's
Hill at Memorial Service for Edward Ulzen (1999)

XXI

My journey to the Netherlands could not have come at a more inopportune time. As the excitement and expectations rose, my wife was undergoing medical investigations for vague symptoms, which turned out to be indicative of a serious illness. This was confirmed the day after I had purchased my ticket to travel to the Netherlands to meet the Black Dutchmen. She reasoned that I could make the trip and return before her surgery, for she had quite rightly guessed that I was ready to abandon the whole idea. "This is too important; if your father were alive, he would have gone in a heartbeat."

So it was that I left North Carolina via Detroit and arrived at Schiphol early on the morning of September 19, 2000. I had always avoided traveling to Ghana via Amsterdam because of the long layover involved for connections to Accra from this airport. I finally found myself at Schiphol. A fine drizzle was in charge of the morning at the airport, and it washed lightly over the airplane and my psychological burdens as we taxied toward the gate. Dr. Van Kessel was sure she would find me without a problem. I had indicated in my e-mail that I was dressed in a beige sports jacket, glasses, and is six feet tall and decidedly as black as Africa.

"Professor Ulzen."

"Dr. Van Kessel."

We bantered a little about my facility with or lack of facility with the

Dutch language. I threw out a not confident mangled phrase from the Dutch language tape I had been hallucinating on for the previous two weeks. Dr. Van Kessel was most unimpressed with my Dutch accent, and thankfully because she spoke good English, I permanently buried my plans to speak Dutch for the coming week. Her husband Johan also spoke good English, so I had little to get neurotic about. Both were of a journalistic background professionally and had visited Africa at various points in the past.

Dr. Van Kessel and I drove through the early morning non-traffic to Leischendam, a journey of about forty minutes. We seemed equally excited about this unlikely meeting and as heavy as my head was, we began to get into various aspects of the history. Leischendam was a nice suburban setting with its village past still barely alive. It was not completely overwhelmed with modernity. Their house was a detached brick home with a wonderful garden stocked with fruits and vegetables, which were well settled in the earth. It was a nature garden with shrubbery and a little stream about halfway up the backyard.

We talked about the plans for the week and also the improbability of our whole meeting. Dr. Van Kessel's mission was, of course, the history of the Java-African soldiers; and I was intrigued by the story but also had a particular curiosity in the Ulzen family tree. I had always hoped to research it as my father had, but never imagined I would be thrust into it in this way.

I was dead tired but alert with anticipation of what I could possibly learn that was new and exciting. Sitting at the kitchen table, facing the garden that was separated from it by a large glass window, I was at once in a new place heading to an old one. We examined documents that Dr. Van Kessel had gathered including a complete list of governors of Elmina. For the first time, I saw the name Roelof Ulzen, Governor from November 4, 1755 to January 15, 1758. His tenure started two hundred years before I was born and ended about two hundred years before Ghana's independence. This finding made it impossible that he was the father of a Java veteran Hermanus Ulzen whose father was noted as Roelof Ulzen in his enlistment documents. A few silent generations were yet to speak to us.

On the table were a number of books related to the yet undefined quest.

An Asante Embassy on the Gold Coast: The mission of Akyempon Yaw to Elmina, 1868–1872, Ashanti and the Dutch, and the novel *Two Hearts of Kwasi Boachi*. The novel told an interesting story of two Ashanti princes sent to the Netherlands at the request of Kwaku Dua, theKing of Ashanti, in 1837. This was ostensibly to cement the state-to-state relationship between the Dutch and the Ashanti Empire after General Verveer's elaborate delegation to Kumasi, the Ashanti capital, in search of recruits for Java.

Rene Baesjou's book was a source of detailed information on the triangular relationship between Elmina, the Dutch, and the Ashanti. The book revealed that at the time of the British takeover of the Elmina Castle in 1872. Manus Ulzen was spokesperson for the free burghers and the No. 10 Asafo Company in Elmina. He would have been sixty years old at the time, having long since returned from Java. The weight of information, jet lag, red wine, and the anticipation of meeting this lost African tribe from Indonesia, now settled in the Netherlands, sent me to sleep for a few hours. Having arrived from the expansive suburbs of America, I found the steps leading to the third floor bedroom where I would sleep in this wonderful home, nearly vertical. In Holland space is in the sky.

I had searched for my kente cloth before the trip and could not find it. This was not unusual. So for the reunion meeting, I decided I would wear a ceremonial smock, *batakari* or *fugu* from Northern Ghana. Dr. Van Kessel and her husband also threw on attires *à l'Africaine* and with the usual assortment of cameras, camcorders, wires, batteries, and the like. We set out for De Rank in Schiedam where the tenth biannual reunion of the Belanda Hitam was scheduled to take place. After a detour through a nearby neighborhood, we finally found our destination. It was raining heavily, as it had done incessantly since I arrived. The sun eventually negotiated its way through the rain intermittently, but the afternoon started out decidedly wet. I really did not know what to expect but was soon met with a diverse group of people who looked mostly Oriental. A few had obvious African features such as their hair than others. People were more or less Oriental in complexion. The hallway was taken up by numerous family photos of men and women now in their seventies and beyond, who pointed themselves out as children in these pictures with great longing in their eyes, hearts, and voices. They also experienced great satisfaction from pointing themselves out and pointing out connections with other people at the gathering and with some that had long since departed. Some pictures of African grandparents and great grandparents were displayed prominently, and I was struck most by that of a man who was clearly from Northern Ghana or Burkina Faso, judging by his facial marks and the distribution of his facial hair. He was the grandfather of Mrs. Cordus. His place of birth was recorded as Sokko, which is apparently just west of Wa in Northern Ghana. I had briefly lived in Wa as a child and remembered those dusty and unbearably hot days of my early childhood well. This was early in my father's career as an education officer in the Ghana Civil Service.

The program was typical as these events go, with the necessary speeches and expressions of gratitude to the organizers. There was a sense that as one generation passed on, the next one might find it harder to be united by the unique past they shared as descendants of African soldiers and Indonesian women. It was a gathering of about 250 people all told. The program included a Ghanaian percussion group from Amsterdam, which did not disappoint in its rendering of pulsating drumming that gave immediate birth to that familiar "what am I doing here?" feeling of homesickness.

After Mr. Daan Cordus opened the event and introduced me as a guest of honor, he also introduced another Belanda Hitam from Chicago who I believe was a cousin of his. Also introduced was a Ghanaian physician from the Netherlands who had also traveled from another city to be at the event. I later found out that this doctor, a Ghanaian journalist covering the event for a local publication, and I were all old students of St. Augustine's College, Cape Coast. That toothless barrier certainly did not keep us on that campus!

XXII

Dr. Van Kessel then began by presenting information she had so far gathered on the African soldiers of the KNIL. She had presented what she had learned about their recruitment and their journeys to the present-day Indonesia. I followed with a short address, which I had penned that morning just before we set out for Schiedam. Dr. Van Kessel provided a sequential translation in Dutch for the audience.

It was more emotional for me than I had imagined it would be. The confluence of my father's death in the preceding eleven months and the lost probability of his near presence, with or without me, added to the realization that my presence represented the first time that the Belanda Hitam had encountered another Belanda Hitam from Africa in the Netherlands. We were but joined as descendants of African soldiers who served in Sumatra and Java. It was a small, diverse, but extremely unique lineage. The circle had been completed. Where would it lead?

As the sole executor of my father's estate, I consulted all the beneficiaries, these being my brother and three sisters, prior to my trip; and we decided that a gift of life to the history of the Java soldiers would be best. We decided that this is probably how our father would have dealt with this situation, for he was a man extremely prone to impromptu donations to causes that were in need or of interest. We offered to house a museum to the history of the Java soldiers at my father's uncompleted house in Elmina. He had always fancied it as a guesthouse and had imagined sharing stories with his guests of his travels and theirs. This is a story he would have died for, but he had already done that.

I began,

> "Ladies and gentlemen of the Belanda Hitam, I am indeed honored to be here today, addressing this special gathering. I begin by expressing my gratitude to Dr. Van Kessel for her hospitality and her interest in the rich history of Africans in the KNIL. I also acknowledge Mr. Daan Cordus with whom I have communicated by e-mail over the last year. Why am I here? I am here because of our shared history. My lamented father Edward Ulzen who departed this world eleven months ago yesterday, would have been here eagerly to discuss this history. He was one of Africa's leading university administrators and an academic in his own right in the field of Adult Education. He was a prince of Elmina. He left a rich legacy of academic excellence and philanthropy. I am here because; in Africa the fact that you are gone doesn't mean you are forgotten. Most of all, I am here because I want to be here. I am here to offer us all an opportunity to complete the circle of history as much as possible. My father's great-grand father, Kpl. Manus Ulzen was a veteran of the KNIL who returned to Elmina in 1835. Apparently, he was a grandson of a Dutch governor of the Elmina Castle. I am also here to announce a gift from the Ulzen families in Ghana, Canada, the UK and USA on behalf of our late lamented patriarch, the late Edward Ulzen. We wish to offer you space in our property in Elmina, as a site for a permanent museum of the history of the courageous and brave fighting men of the Belanda Hitam. We give this gift, with the expectation that our shared history will move from the archives in Holland and Indonesia to Elmina where the African sun will shine on the stories of our lives. I hope this will encourage all of you, at some point to visit Elmina, not as strangers but as returning sons and daughters of Ghana. We say. Sankofa…

There is virtue in seeking one's roots. Thank you very much, Hartle Dank."

The gathering responded with enthusiastic applause, but I could not tell if it was out of politeness or emotion. Dr. Van Kessel later told me from my asking about the audience's response, that for a Dutch gathering, the response was effusive and unrestrained.

Many themes arose from the numerous conversations I had that day. One jazz music lover, a man in his fifties, who looked quite fair in complexion, almost Indo-European in appearance, expressed his embarrassment at not knowing his history. He did say he now understood that his love of jazz must be instinctive for he was an African at the core of his being. A young man in his twenties, rather Negroid for all his Asiatic genes, came toward me with his mother. He was emotional and spoke with great feeling about how deprived he had felt. Their father knew of his family's African lineage but only shared it on his deathbed. He shared it as a fact, depriving them of the knowledge he had of it. Then there was the old lady I sat next to for a while as the dancing went on. The crowd came alive as a very typical Indonesian dance with parasols took over the event. This dance seemed to be from the forties or fifties, and the older generation went berserk with the music and dance of their Asian homeland. As the couples danced in pairs with their parasols, she shared with me a story her grandmother often told of her grandfather, an African. "My grandfather was an African," she said with a healthy excitement. He was apparently often homesick and would get quite melancholic. When he got sad, he would take out his African drum and beat it incessantly, but the message was not heard in Africa. He would be in tears; and his wife would go to the garden, harvest some of the produce, and make him *okro* stew. This somehow brought him home, and he would settle down after this African delicacy was served up.

I was back with the young man with African features. He continued his story. He felt that his father had deprived them of their life stories and the meanings of these stories all went with him. He felt robbed and put it eloquently to his mother, "This man is offering us a choice, an open door; it is up to us to walk through it to discover our past in Africa." He spoke of being in school in Indonesia during the '70s. The other children would call him "Kunta Kinte" from Alex Haley's *Roots* epic because of his African features. He thought little of it until the events of his father's demise when he discovered why others thought he looked African in some way. That is when it all came alive in his consciousness.

As the night wore on, the Indonesian dance from the fifties continued. The couples danced a waltz under the parasols. It was a most graceful dance, reminding me of my own favorite Ghanaian dance *Takai* from Dagbon. They were similar in their grace and unhurried tempo. It also then struck me that many of the ancestors of the people gathered were from Northern Ghana or Burkina Faso via Kumasi and then Elmina to the East Indies.

As I was absorbing all of this, having been defeated by spicy Indonesian foods, sweet desserts, and cold beer for a few unrelenting hours, the elderly woman who had told me about her grandfather and his drum started telling me about her joint pains. She tried to get me to sort out her prescriptions. I was amused because I thought, for the first time in years, I would be at a party and not have to do anything medical. How wrong I had been. I kept thinking about her grandfather who had died before she was born and of the tears streaming down his face as he drummed and drummed and drummed to no avail. But somehow, the fruits of his garden healed him.

For Mr. Cordus, my presence at this event was a dream of a lifetime. His search for Africa had led to an open door through the Ulzen family of Elmina, the town through which his grandfather had sailed to the East Indies. He was preparing to travel to Ghana for the first time and looked forward to seeing Kumasi, from which city his journey would begin along the road his grandfather must have traveled on foot to Elmina. This journey of four hours today was a twelve-day journey by foot in those days. We planned to meet in Ghana, as I was to visit in October for the commemoration of the first anniversary of my father's passing.

XXIII

I spent some time on touristic pursuits. A walk through Leiden, an old and beautiful city with a story of pilgrims to the United States buried in its soul. It also hid a photo of Dr. Kofi Abrefa Busia, a former Prime Minister of Ghana, who had taught there. Mr. Cordus also took me on a tame tour of Amsterdam, as he noted its extreme liberalism and the pursuit of Dionysus. It was a fleeting diversion from my worries about my wife's illness and impending surgery. The excitement of the hunt for new information about my family kept me invigorated nonetheless. I had no ultimate endpoint on the search for all Ulzens, but information seemed to find me. This was not without the efforts of Dr. Van Kessel, who informed a few key individuals of my visit and its various facets.

After a few days of telephone tag Dr. Van Kessel finally caught up with Natalie Everts, a doctoral candidate who had been studying relationships between African women and European men in eighteenth and nineteenth century Elmina. This was during the period of the European prominence on the Guinea coast and the period of unrestrained raping of the land for slaves.

"Yes!" She knew the Ulzen name and had a great deal of information on Roelof Ulsen the ex-governor of Dutch Guinea. He had married an African woman in his time. We confirmed a meeting time. We walked along briskly through the afternoon showers to Miss Everts's department.

Dr. Van Kessel and I found her after trudging down a few corridors. She was expecting us, but I found her somewhat flustered as we went through the usual pleasantries. She was not offensive in any way. She just seemed to have another train of thought going. She was a dark-haired woman, maybe in her late thirties, seated behind her desk in a somewhat characterless office. It looked like a library without books. I handed her my card, and she gave the tiniest gasp, seeming a little emotional as she read my full name, Thaddeus Patrick Manus Ulzen. She then explained that she had a book on Roelof Ulsen written by an amateur historian, one Mr. Van Zoest from Brielle where Roelof Ulsen was born. She began to share the story, as she understood it, with us but was going to provide other documents she had. At this point, it became clear that there was something in Roelof Ulsen's dealings with The Hague that was probably scandalous at some level, and she felt some discomfort in discussing this. Rather than go into the whole story, she seemed to lean more toward my reading the book and gathering the story for myself.

Roelof had accompanied his father as a boy of about ten years of age to Elmina in 1732. His father Jan Ulsen had lost both his wife and his son Johannes and was essentially a single parent. In 1730, Jan Ulsen was a sergeant in the company of the Lord La Coragie. This company was probably part of the Regiment Nationalen established in 1602, later named Saint Amant and Wolterus. This regiment was frequently stationed in Brielle, which explains how Jan Ulsen met Maria van Keulen, who hailed from an aristocratic Brielle family. In Brielle, the couple lived in Zevenhuizen (a row of seven houses on one side of the harbor). On February 7, 1720, a son Johannes was baptized in the Groote Kerk in Brielle. His godparents were Johannes Vieroot and Cecilia van Keulen.

Jan Ulsen was posted in 1731 as Vaandrig of Fort St. Jago, on the hill in Elmina, north of the castle. Tragically, he died within a year of his arrival in Elmina. The archives of the West India Company (WIC) reveal in a dispatch from Governor Jan Pranger to the West India Company on August 1, 1731, "We have stationed Vaandrig Jan Ulsen and his son Rulof Ulsen on St. Jago Hill."

Travel to faraway new lands is often spurred on by personal crises from which one walks away or flees. Sometimes it is a mere retreat to strengthen ones resolve to return to confront the original problem. It is not a fast trot; it is a steady and deliberate walk. In this case, it was a slow journey by sea to a continent unknown to this soldier. This story reminded me of my own father's departure from Ghana in August 1967 after he lost his job and his marriage. He lived outside his beloved native Ghana for twenty-six years. So Jan Ulsen arrived at Fort St. Jago with his son Roelof just as we arrived in Lusaka with our father in 1967. We do not know what Jan Ulsen's motivations were, but it was unusual in those days for a single man to receive custody of a child, and even more unusual to take one's son to the proverbial "white man's grave" in Guinea! To gain custody of his son, he promised "to raise his child honestly and properly, both with regard to food and clothing and education, to send him to school and to have him learn a proper trade, until the age of 25 years or the date of marriage."

His tragic death soon after his arrival in Elmina, a branch office of "the white man's grave," left his young son a veritable orphan. Vaandrig Jan Ulsen destined his son to a future in Africa by making a deathbed request that his colleagues keep and look after the boy on the coast. The WIC records dated December 14, 1732, indicate,

> "With regard to the surviving son of the late Vaandrig Ulsen I can respond that his father shortly before his death had asked me and Oppercommies Elet to accept supervision over the aforementioned young man as long as we will be stationed on the Coast, and to appoint someone else for this purpose in case of our departure or death. This we have promised the dying man. Meanwhile the aforementioned Oppercommies (Elet) has sent him to Accra, where he is placed under the supervision of an elderly person, and kept well disciplined."

No mention is made of the boy's loss, his grief, or matters of that nature. In those days, children were seen but not heard, so their emotions were fictional in the minds of adults.

Governor Jan Pranger and Oppercommies Elet were his mentor and guardian respectively. Young Roelof grew up on the coast, eventually becoming *oppercommies* or chief merchant of the Dutch West India Company in 1753. The main commerce at this time was slavery, and no merchant on the coast survived without being immersed in this sordid business. He worked for the WIC just as his father had done and rose through the WIC ranks as a European raised on the Gold Coast of West Africa. It is not known who his significant adult figures were beyond the two WIC officials who carried out his father's wishes. A statement that he had served the WIC for twenty-nine years accompanied his passport issued at the end of his WIC service in 1764. His service then must have begun in 1735, when he was fourteen years old as a cadet. He was eleven years old when his father died.

By the time Roelof Ulsen became Governor of Dutch Elmina in 1755, the trade routes in the interior had dried up because of the defiance of the western and other southern states against the dominant inland power, the Ashanti. His predecessor, Director – General N. M. van Nood de Gietere, had launched a peace initiative after Fanti chiefs from the south had failed to secure an agreement between the Ashanti and the rebellious nations of Wassa, Denkyira, Twifo, and Akyem. Two Elmina men of Dutch employ, Dwumo and Andafo, were the emissaries who carried out this diplomatic initiative.

During these negotiations to avert a full-scale war, Director – General N. M. van der Nood de Gietere died and was succeeded by Roelof Ulsen. He persisted with the peace initiative through his intermediaries and was able to negotiate a payment of one thousand *bendas* of gold as a sign of good faith from the rebels. This was part of an eight-point piece plan, which the rebels eventually rejected after initial indications that peace would prevail. They were later prepared to lose their one thousand bendas of gold, of which only eight hundred had been paid. The rebels further detained the Ashanti ambassador Mensah while the African emissaries of Roelof Ulsen returned to Elmina for further consultations.

The emissaries, Dwuomo and Kofi Andafo, servants respectively of van der Nood de Gietere and Ulsen, returned to Roelof Ulsen with gifts from the Ashanti for his efforts. Osei Kojo was the king of Ashanti at this time. This was so even though the Ashantis had received only eight hundred of the promised one thousand bendas of gold from the rebels. Before the treaty could be finalized, the rebels declared they would rather die in battle than accept the Ashanti terms for peace.

By 1758, it was clear that the initiative had failed to secure peace and, hence, the security of the trade routes from Ashanti to the coast. The rebellious states had flouted all conventions of decency among the Akan nations. Their actions included harassing and beheading Ashanti traders on free roads. These wanton acts culminated in the death of a herald dispatched by the king of Ashanti to inquire into the hostilities. This amounted to a de facto state of war. The net result of these hostilities was a halt to trade in slaves and goods between the Ashanti and the Dutch on the coast at Elmina.

This period of turmoil began in 1744, during the reign of Kwasi Obodum of Ashanti. He was an elderly king who had succeeded his nephew, the great Opoku Ware I. He was in turn, succeeded in 1752 by Osei Kojo. This king was preoccupied with expansion to the north, where he subdued the Dagomba and imposed an annual tribute of slaves and livestock, which remained in force until 1874. He was, however, unable to assert his control over the Fantis till the end of his reign in 1781. This period of unrest along the coast created anxiety among the Europeans about the worsening inland trade. This ultimately led to the conflict between the Ashanti and the British, after the Ashantis defeated the Fantis in 1806.

On October 11, 1755, van Nood de Gietere completed the first comprehensive written contract codifying the relationship between the Dutch and people of Elmina, formalizing what had been in place informally since the 1730s. This contract established the role of the Dutch as judicial partners with the chiefs, heads of the Asafo companies, and the Elmina grandes, caboceers or wealthy men. It covered trade but also judicial arrangements between the WIC and Elmina's leaders, stressing mechanisms for peace and good order. After an association of over a century, the rules of shared governance over the city-state were finally recorded. Roelof Ulsen, who had a deep understanding of the coast and who became Governor of the coast from November 4, 1755 – January 15, 1758, would have played a significant role in these developments and was the first

Dutch administrator to effectively administer the agreement. This "Pen and Contract" agreement formed the basis of future agreements in 1769, 1762, 1780, 1786 and 1796.

Roelof Ulsen received the following gifts in 1758 for his role in the failed attempts at peacemaking:

1.	From King "Quisie"	1 gold armband (2oz.) and 2 boy slaves at 1/2 man.
2.	From Danqua	1 elderly woman slave and one girl.
3.	From Safo Kantanka	1 elderly man slave.
4.	From "Essantifor"	1 man slave, young and well.
5.	Akjaanba (King's Aunt)	1 fine small Ashanti cloth.
6.	Ambassador Mensah	1 boy 1/3 man

Gifts to other principals of Elmina included

1.	Subfactor van Bakergem (Son of van der Nood de Gietere)	1 youth at ½ man
2.	Caboceer Endubiansan	1 man slave
3.	Caboceer Jaken	1 youth at ½ man
4.	Caboceer Dwumo	1 man slave and 1 youth at ½ man

Other Elmina grandes who received gifts of gold and/or slaves included caboceers Corantier, Eijniakon, and Kweku Eijnin. Notably absent from the recipient list are the chiefs of Elmina. During this period, the wealthy brokers or caboceers held most of the political power within the African community in Elmina.

1742 portrait of Jan Pranger Governor of Elmina (March 1730 – March 1734) with permission Rijksmuseum, Amsterdam

Java Hill: An African Journey

Sevenhuizen – Birth place of Roelof Ulsen (Governor, Elmina Castle 01/1756 – 04/1758) in Brielle, Netherlands

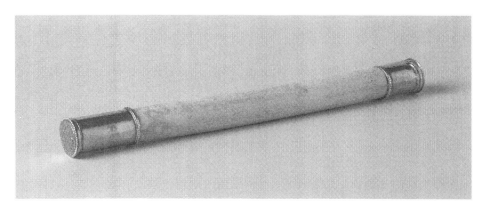

Commando Staf (Staff of Office of Governor, Elmina Castle), with permission Rijksmuseum, Amsterdam

Signature of Roelof Ulsen 1764 (Brielle Archives)

XXIV

This was a busy period on the Gold Coast with European powers blatantly locking horns to secure suzerainty on the coast. In 1757, the French made a bold but unsuccessful attempt to capture Cape Coast Castle, the British stronghold twelve miles east of Elmina. Cape Coast became the capital of the later British colony of the Gold Coast, which eventually became the Republic of Ghana. European powers were scheming at a frenzied pace to deepen their involvement in the slave trade without exception. In the history of this period written by European powers, the frenzied level of greed and the extreme militarization of the coast, which exponentially fuelled the slave trade in many areas and initiated it in others, are not well emphasized.

During the eighteenth century, the relationships between the Dutch and the people of Elmina underwent considerable change. Trade continued to be the primary focus of the relationship, but it was inevitable that the Dutch and the people of Elmina would have to develop new structures of governance to protect their mutual advantages in trade. The Dutch retained an African who served as an ambassador to other African states in the region, vital to the trade in gold, fabrics, slaves, and other items. This person was known as the *makelaar*. The first such *makelaar* of record was Akim, who served until 1702. During the century, there were six makelaars of note. Their respective tenures are not consistently recorded in the written history of Elmina. As best as we know, they were Pieter Passop from 1703,

Abocan to 1737, Amba from 1741 to 1748, Quow Mysang (Ekow Mensah) from 1767 to the 1780s, and Quammena in the 1790s.

The most colorful makelaar was Abocan, who had a private army, which he placed at the disposal of the Dutch from time to time for military expeditions and also civil projects, such as the repair of roads. He also owned a fleet of boats as well as a small salt village. He had direct access to the governor and could imprison kidnapped persons who owed him money at St. George's Castle. Against Dutch reservations, he was able to get his nominee, Tekki (Takyi), appointed as under-*makelaar;* but when Tekki was found guilty of plotting to murder Abocan, he persuaded the Dutch to exile him to Surinam. His great wealth and closeness to the Ashanti was a great source of resentment among the neighboring Fanti. Only later in the eighteenth century did the office of *Ohen* (chief or king) of Elmina gain any prominence.

In 1702, Elmina could boast of twelve thousand fighting men who constituted the beginnings of the Asafo companies. However, following the smallpox epidemic and the Komenda Wars, the number of fighting men was generally estimated to be between three thousand and five thousand. The Dutch operated by upholding Akan customary law and often found themselves required to settle disputes between the Asafo companies. There was a particularly protracted conflict between two companies, Abesi and Allade, which continued from 1757 to 1760. Governor Huydecoper, who threatened to fire cannon into the town from Fort San Jago, finally settled this conflict. In 1764, there was another conflict between Enyampa and Allade on one hand and the other Asafo companies on the other. The Dutch were invested in the Asafo companies as they had relied on them in military sorties against such adversaries as John Conny in 1724 and during the Fante-Elmina conflicts of 1725, 1738, and 1740.

Asafo companies, as they are now called, were essentially organized regiments of young men who performed civic duties and functioned as the de facto army of Elmina. They were not unique to Elmina but were a regular feature of Fante-speaking coastal towns. Trade, brought in many outsiders and the Asafo companies, evolved from the increasingly cosmopolitan nature of Elmina. The first companies grew out of immigrants from Denkyira and Akyem. Young men generally joined their fathers' companies. Asafo companies were also created for slaves and paid hands from the Slave Coast, which required a social method for interacting with the larger society. They were either absorbed into their masters' companies or into a special company for migrant workers of the Dutch, which in the nineteenth century was the No. 9 Company, the Marowafo. From the late nineteenth century, Elmina has been organized into ten Asafo "quarters." Over the centuries, these companies have had many functions in society other than their obvious military role, in defense of the state.

The members of the No. 7 Company, Enyampa, elect the king of Elmina, who must be a member of either the Nsona or Anona royal family. At the time of his death, my father, Nanabanyin Edward Ulzen, was the captain (Vaandrig) of this company. This title is inherited on the principle of patrilineality, similar to Elmina chieftaincy itself. Hermanus Ulzen of Java was spokesperson for No.10, known then as the free burghers and now as Akrampafo. Their leader was known as the Burgomaster. The head of all the companies was known as the Groot Vaandrig or the great ensign. He is always selected from the No. 3 Company. Elmina originally had seven Asafo companies or army units. Two were added in the nineteenth century. No. 8 was made up of refugees from Eguafo and Simbo during the Fante war of 1810. No. 9 was made up mostly of the descendants of former WIC servants or *landslaven*. Through the Asafo companies, the popular voice of the people was always heard. It formed an ill-defined sort of parliament. Young men also ended up with their fathers' professions through these companies. They were usually fishermen, farmers, or craftsmen. The companies, therefore, also served as a means of production in the community.

Though the Dutch had been in Elmina since 1637, and previous agreements existed consistently from 1732, their relationship with the leaders of the town was not fully formalized until 1755 at the end of the directorship of N. M. van der Nood de Gietere. He was Roelof Ulsen's immediate predecessor as governor. On October 11, 1755, the agreement, known as the "pen and contract," between the Dutch and the people Elmina was concluded with significant financial enhancements. During this year, the Asafo ward or quarter leaders were formally recognized with the payment of *kostgeld* as official representatives of the town. The leader of all the Asafo companies was first recognized as the Groot Vaandrig or great ensign in 1741. For example, in 1765, Jacon the Groot Vaandrig received as *kostgeld* of one ounce of gold per month. The Groot Vaandrig participated in dispute resolution within Elmina society and also in the resolution of problems, which occurred between the Dutch and the people of Elmina. The pen and contract was an agreement which set out guidelines for deciding which disputes were handled according to Akan customary law and which ones came under the jurisdiction of the Dutch at Elmina Castle. Having grown up on the coast, Roelof Ulsen, who was then oppercommies or chief merchant, contributed his understanding of the role of the Asafo companies in governance to the decision by his predecessor to formalize the role of these young men in 1755. Under the agreement, the most severe of punishment for an offense, including murder, was exile to Surinam.

The king of Elmina or Ohen generally heard civil cases involving his citizens and the town. Sometimes for political expediency, some of these cases were referred to the Dutch, particularly when the king felt that leaving the decision to the Dutch was likely to result in the desired outcome. Cases involving mulattos were generally brought to Elmina Castle under Dutch jurisdiction. Where mulattos were concerned, the judicial systems were often in conflict because of their mixed parentage and heritage. This was especially contentious when inheritance was the issue. An example involves the case of the wealthy merchant, Jacob Vandyke, who is my father's ancestor on the maternal line. The day before he died, he recorded a will by the first clerk of the West Indies Company with witnesses present. He designated his son as heir and appointed three Dutch officials as executors of his estate and guardians to his son. This went against Akan customary law, which dictated that he should have appointed a maternal nephew or cousin as his heir. His death was followed by a protracted conflict, which included a siege of his home. The Dutch governor eventually prevailed; and European law was upheld in this particular case, making his son, Peter Vandyke, his legal heir. Most mulattos married Africans, which made this type of conflict common, particularly when a large estate was at stake. The grave of Peter Vandyke ("Ewulman") who died in 1882 is still marked in the Dutch cemetery in Elmina to the present day. He was the grandson of the wealthy merchant Jacob Vandyke of the 18th century. His father was most likely Pieter Vandyke who was born in 1740 and lived in the Netherlands until the age of twenty-one. His mother was Nana Nyanyiwa after whom my father's maternal family is named.

Vandyke and Cornelis House in Elmina – Built by Jacob Ruhle an engineer in 1897. Part of this house was sold to Mr. Vandyke, a lawyer and author of the Elmina (Edina) State Constitution. He is a maternal ancestor of the Ulzen's of Sybil, Elmina

View of Elmina Castle from Sybil, Elmina

Java Hill: An African Journey

Maternal Family Tree of Ulzens of Sybil, Elmina

XXV

After Roelof Ulsen's term as governor ended in 1758, he continued to live in Elmina, which had essentially been his home since he had arrived with his father in 1731. His continued presence in Elmina was a source of concern for officials succeeding him since he was, for all practical purposes, a local African. His loyalty to anyone other than himself was suspect. Life among the Dutch officials on the coast was dreary; alcohol, disease, and death filled. Their dreadful lives were moderated only by the illicit and formal relationships with African women along the coast. The story of J. P. T. Huydecoper is but one example of such a life on the Guinea coast.

J. P. T. Huydecoper was a young man from a prominent Dutch family, who was deeply in debt from his own waywardness. He arrived on the coast in 1756, during the directorship of Roelof Ulsen, hoping to make a fortune on what was politely known as the coastal trade. He expected to be appointed governor because of his family connections in the Netherlands. His uncle, Balthasar Huydecoper, had been the mayor of Amsterdam. On arrival, he assumed the rank of oppercommies (chief merchant) of Dutch Guinea at the age of twenty-eight. This was the second highest rank in the WIC hierarchy, and a few heads must have turned. This was a harsh environment. Of the ninety new personnel who arrived on the same ship with Huydecoper, one third died within two months.

In no time, he had a public confrontation with Roelof Ulsen who, being an old hand, had apparently been undermining J. P. T. Huydecoper, whose eagerness to be appointed governor must have been a source of irritation to the more seasoned WIC officials on the coast. Roelof Ulsen, though no longer governor, continued to serve as a member of the council of six, in charge of the North and South Coast of Africa. This council functioned as a court of law. He appeared to retain considerable influence in the Dutch hierarchy in Elmina and must have found Huydecoper an upstart who had not paid his dues.

In a published memoir, based on correspondence with his family, J. P. T. Huydecoper renders a damning account of how Roelof Ulsen, with whom he had placed his trust and viewed as a mentor, had betrayed him. Upon the death of Ulsen's secretary, Huydecoper found correspondence from Ulsen portraying Huydecoper in very negative light. Having been confronted with the written evidence, Ulsen had no choice but to apologize and attempt to make amends. J. P. T. Huydecoper would not be appeased. He evicted Ulsen from his lodgings at the Elmina Castle. He clearly saw Ulsen as a rival for the position of governor because it was not unusual for a former governor to be reappointed. This would have interfered with the J. P. T. Huydecoper's plans to become governor, make money in the slave trade and pay off his massive debts in the Netherlands. He writes to his family in the Netherlands that the old hands are corrupt and only interested in booze, sex, and tobacco. He confirms, "The Ten commandments do not apply south of the Equator." Elmina, though, lies north of the equator, but his meaning is clear. In 1764, the Dutch Reformed Minister Gerardus Verbeet complains about how immoral life is on the coast among the Europeans. He decides to send his wife back to Europe while he notes that "conditions are such that no married women can live here in happiness, there being no other woman who confesses the Christian religion." He adds, "Whites have taken a 'heathen' as concubine and even boast that they have two or three children born out of these relationships. These children grow up as heathens and remain intentionally unbaptized, in order to give them to other whites as extramarital partners." In 1766, Huydecoper informs the WIC in another dispatch that the "drunk schoolmaster Bogaard has been found drowned in brandy. He was found dead on the floor of his house, with brandy still flowing from his mouth."

His appointment as governor was not to occur immediately as L. Jacob van Tets was appointed governor in succession to Roelof Ulsen. Huydecoper felt humiliated at apparently being bypassed in spite of his blatant lobbying for the position. He needn't have worried as Van Tets's tenure was brief. He succeeded Van Tets as governor later in 1758. Two years later, in 1760, he was relieved of his command and transferred west to Fort St. Anthony in Axim, which was reputed to be a desolate and boring posting. His tenure as governor had been turbulent and caused a great deal of tension. He now suffered the frightening fate of having to travel by night to his new station in an open canoe. His ambition to make a quick fortune was not achieved because, even though he sold a lot of slaves, he was paid in merchandise and had to find a way of converting his earnings to cash to pay off his debts. He had, by this time, become involved with a mulatto woman, Penni Raems, with whom he later had a daughter Barbara. While in Axim, his daughter died in Elmina. He was lonely and could not share his immense grief with anyone, especially his family in Holland who did not know he had another family on the coast. He confided in Governor Erasmi but was unsure of his fidelity. In keeping with customary European practice on the coast, he kept his African family life secret from his family in Holland. His fortunes changed for the better after he was finally reappointed governor in 1764. By this time, his mulatto wife Penni Raems had given birth to a son Willem. He now had a greater sense of purpose in his life but could still not share any of this with his family and friends in Holland. Sadly, Penni Raems died in 1765 in the seventh year of their relationship. His grief was infinite. He gave her what amounted to a state funeral. It is described as one of the most memorable funerals in Elmina, capped with nine minutes of cannon fire from the castle in her honor. She was effectively the first lady of Elmina and was given final rites consistent with her status, informal as it may have been.

Huydecoper had already secretly spirited off Jan Sprogel, Penni's son from a previous liaison, to Holland for an education at a cost of six hundred guilders per year. This was not an insignificant amount as his salary was roughly three hundred florins per month. A slave from Whydah on the Slave Coast was purchased for about three florins. The WIC officers were poorly paid and, as a result, were generally corrupt and were more interested in their own properties and private businesses to the detriment of the company. He had planned to send his son Willem to the Netherlands in the future, but this was not to be as he died in 1767 with two wills, one for his family in Elmina and the other for his family in Holland. He is known to have had two sons with two other women in Elmina apart from Penni Raems.

Roelof Ulsen asked to be dismissed from WIC service in 1760 but stayed on the coast until 1764. He was eventually issued a passport on October 26, 1764, for his return to the Netherlands, a country his eyes had not seen for about thirty years. It appears that he was in no hurry to leave Africa and that his conflicts with Huydecoper had probably set the stage for his eventual departure. Huydecoper had been acting governor after the death of Van Tets, but this period was noted to have been quite disturbing to the extent that when Peter Erasmi died, the WIC was reluctant to reappoint Huydecoper. He is noted to have threatened workers, saying to the bookkeeper, "Shut up or I'll kick you out of the room." He is also accused of causing indebtedness to the company and waging a costly war in Axim.

By 1763, Roelof Ulsen appears to have regained Huydecoper's trust. "He (Ulsen) is now again held in the highest esteem and is acting as mentor of our president (governor)." A party is held to mark the restoration of the friendship between the two men. Huydecoper sends a report in which he points out that the officials on the coast believed that one cannot enjoy oneself without being drunk, and they all indulge in this practice. The following describes a typical evening: "When evening falls, one official (the *fiscaal*) slips quietly away to go home. The others do not accept this, and follow him to his house to persuade him to rejoin the party. The fiscaal receives them hospitably, and there is more tasting of wine. Alcohol revives the spirits and a conflict erupts about the professional qualities of the surgeon Miltz and the pharmacist Ravesteijn, who have a known history of rivalry between them. With all the alcohol consumption, everybody becomes over excited. Huydecoper remarks to a colleague that he has the powers to have the other locked away until he is sober. This incident spoils the party, so everybody decides to leave the house and go for the evening meal. The fiscaal now starts crying, but then the others return to collect him. People shake hands, the trumpet player is called, somebody plays the violin and the partygoers start dancing."

As Huydecoper explains to his superiors, "These things happen when there is too much drinking during parties." During his own governorship, one of the officials had become so drunk that he found the courage to grab the wig from Huydecoper's head and hit him with the wig in the face. Huydecoper signs the letter reporting this incident as "your humble, faithful, but thus far unhappy servant." Life on the coast had its challenges.

XXVI

Roelof Ulsen set sail for Rotterdam in 1764 to continue his association with Coopstad & Rochussen, a shipping line in which he was a partner. This company was like all others at the time, directly involved in the slave trade (1740–1790). Before Roelof Ulsen leaves, he seeks freedom for two African women, who are apparently his wife and daughter. The record shows that he ensures their freedom in Elmina prior to his departure.

> "We Mr. J. P. T. Huydecoper Director General etc. appointed as such by the honorable excellencies of the States - General, for all who will read this to be greeted and to know that the honorable Roelof Ulsen, formerly president on this coast, just prior to his departure to Europa has requested from us with all due respect, to declare the Negro woman named Aquisiba Adjewa Braffoe and her daughter Johanna both free persons and to provide to them with our open letters, as he has purchased their freedom from their owner, the Negro woman Abbeba, by giving her two female slaves, this done in our presence. Therefore, acting on your sovereign authority which we are honored to represent here, as we find nothing unfair in this request, we hereby declare the aforementioned Aquisiba Adjewa Braffoe and her daughter Johanna from now on to be free and to be liberated from all servile obligations. We authorize her to accept estates,

to make a testament, to govern her own properties and businesses end to enjoy all the privileges, which come with the status of free persons, just as if they were born free. We request all our successors to safeguard this decision and demand that these open letters be respected, in order to do justice to our decision. . Thus stated in the main Castle St. George d'Elmina on 13th Oct. 1764."

By this time, Roelof Ulsen was a man of some means, and as a partner in the shipping company, simply loaded his belongings on board the *Publicola* without an accurate inventory. He was expected to pay his freight costs on arrival in Rotterdam. He had no close family in the Netherlands. According to the account from Aire van Zoest, the amateur historian in Brielle, the ship finally sails from Elmina on October 26, 1764. On board is Roelof Ulsen, his "natural son" Hermanus, four Negro servants, and thirty-two cargo slaves. On the account of the shipping company, the ship carries a further 304 cargo slaves plus fourteen cargo slaves on the account of a D. Kloekenaar, all with destination Surinam where they are to meet a uniformly inhuman fate. The number of crew is not mentioned.

The property of N. M. van der Nood de Gietere, who was earlier deceased, are part of Ulsen's cargo ostensibly for delivery to the dead man's next of kin in Holland. Among Ulsen's possessions on board was a chest with tobacco, a chest with liquor, a table, tableware, chinaware, a bed (beneath it is a chest with gold dust), guns and pistols, a desk, and other items. He has the use of several rooms on board the ship. For young Hermanus, a sleeping couch was prepared in the cabin.

Meals were served everyday according to the wishes of Roelof Ulsen. Every day he had rice soup with salted lentils. His Negro servants prepared "pons" (a punch) from lemon juice, brandy, sugar, and water. Ulsen is depicted as a generous man; he often handed out wine, pons, and coffee to the crew and the officers.

The main problem on the journey was the drunkenness of the chief navigator. At one point, he landed totally drunk on the deck of the cargo slaves, and also attempted to get the crew drunk.

On the trip, one develops a sense of Roelof Ulsen as a living contradiction.

Granted he is a man in the 1760s and living both as an African and a European on the West Coast of Africa. He generously provided alcohol to the crew, who sailed in a drunken chaos with intractable arguments between the captain and the navigator. He, however, replaced one of his dead cargo slaves with one of his four African servants who had apparently not served him to his satisfaction. Thirteen slaves died en route to Surinam on the *Publicola*.

On December 21, 1764, the *Publicola* arrived in South America. Roelof disembarked with his son and spent two days as the guest of a local commissar, Mr. Steenberg. Two of his servants also accompanied them, and one servant stayed on board to watch his belongings, the fourth one having been earlier converted into an article of commerce. The slaves were sold for 130 guilders per head to an inhuman fate in Surinam. The cargo slaves had now reached their destination. Of the 304 cargo slaves, twelve died en route plus one slave from Ulsen's cargo. On instructions given by Ulsen, Captain Van Bell purchased more merchandise. Almost three months later, on March 13, 1765, the *Publicola* sails from Surinam to Holland with new cargo. The menu was again soup and salted lentils, pons, wine and coffee.

When they finally set sail for Rotterdam, Ulsen was intermittently unwell but was up and about. At 4:00 a.m. on the fifteenth of May 1765, he died suddenly as his illness, short as it was, transcended anything that could be done for him. This, of course, created a significant problem as everyone tried to shield little Hermanus from the trauma of the sudden loss of his father. Roelof Ulsen died in the presence of one of the crewmembers, a third witness (Leendert Wuijster), and the Negro servants. The corpse was prepared according to shipping customs with only shirt and trousers remaining on the body.

The captain consulted on what was to be done. Should they place the body in a coffin and take it to Holland or put it in a coffin for a burial at sea? As the voyage may still be long and the ship already carried fifteen sick people, it was decided that Ulsen be buried at sea. A coffin was manufactured from the best wood available; at sunrise, the flags were set at half-mast and a shot was fired every hour. The coffin was loaded with some sandbags and bullets to make sure it met the earth under the ocean. The coffin was then carried on the shoulders of six officers and put on a shelf. While all the canons were fired and the flags of mourning hoisted, the coffin was lowered overboard. Then the regular flags were raised again. Meanwhile, Hermanus remained in his cabin with one of the Negro servants, to prevent him from getting upset. The assistant navigator then sealed all of Ulsen's properties. The chief navigator was unable to be present since he was totally drunk and was throwing up.

The Negro servant Berij (or Pichem) then pointed out which two bottles of gold dust belonged to Ulsen and which two bottles belonged to the shipping company. The captain wanted this to be done in the presence of the other officers so that they will know what belongs to the shipping company in case the captain himself dies before arrival in Holland.

As far as is known, Ulsen did not keep any written records. His wine cellar consisted of fifty bottles of Madeira wine. However, his own consumption on board ship and his treats to the crew did not come from his own stocks but from the stock of the ship. The consumption amounted to seven "ankers" wine and 1.5 "ockshoofd" (both ancient measures of liquid) beer to be paid by Ulsen after arrival in Rotterdam.

On June 7, 1765, about three weeks after Roelof Ulsen's death and burial at sea, the *Publicola* arrives at Rotterdam with a little African boy not quite recognized legally as a person. He accompanied his European father's belongings, his father's servants, darker than he, and the belongings of van der Nood de Gietere, a deceased Dutch governor from the Guinea coast. Hermanus' fate was in the hands of hungry and destitute distant white relatives, most of whom had no real knowledge of or relationship with his father.

The irony of Roelof Ulsen's life was that in the end, his body traveled to the bottom of the Atlantic Ocean just like many of the African slaves who did not survive the treacherous journey to the New World. His son Hermanus, probably about ten years old at the time, was shielded from seeing his father's body travel to the bottom of the Atlantic. Not anticipating his own untimely death, Roelof Ulsen had not kept an inventory of all the items he had on board. As a result, there was no simple way of establishing ownership of the various items.

He had no direct kin in the Netherlands. However, his closest identified relatives mushroomed onto the scene to make a claim to the estate. He had died without making a will. No member of the family offered to look after little Hermanus. Ironically, it was his business partner and co-slave trader, Herman Coopstad, who advocated that 10 percent of the estate be set aside for the boy and that the interest derived from these funds be used to educate Hermanus in the Netherlands.

In Rotterdam, Hendrik Sluijter, an agent of Coopstad & Rochussen, came on board; and in the presence of several witnesses (including Hermanus and the Negro servant Berij), the chest with gold dust was opened. Sluijter takes possession of the two bottles, which belong to the shipping company and then the chest is sealed again. Ulsen's goods are stored in the warehouse of Coopstad & Rochussen. Already on June 8, Herman Coopstad stated in a notarized document that the deceased had no known relatives. He noted that Coopstad & Rochussen will make an inventory of the estate and look after the goods in the interest of little Hermanus. Coopstad took custody of Hermanus.

Soon after, the Vieroot brothers arrived with a court order in which they were designated the likely heirs of Roelof Ulsen who died without leaving a will. A Johannes Vieroot was the godfather of Roelof's deceased brother Johannes, who died as an infant. The Vieroots appear to have been relatives by marriage from his maternal family, the Van Keulens. The goods were handed to them, even though the basis of their claim to the estate was not entirely clear. After some discussion, the brothers donated the table, the silverware, and the bed to Captain Van Bell. However, the captain disposed of the bed the same evening because of a terrific stench. The liquor was still on board as it could only be imported with an excise permit. The captain told the Vieroot brothers that if they wanted the alcohol, they would have to drink it all on board, after which, the brothers decided to leave it behind. Among Ulsen's possessions was also a "commando staf" (staff of office).

For the amount of fifteen guilders, all the goods were shipped to Amsterdam. This included various chests, desks, liquor containers, chests with mirrors, bags, a barrel of coffee beans, lemon juice, guns, pistols, etc. A quarrel erupted about some possessions, which remained on board, notably the silverware. At some point, Captain Van Bell was arrested in Amsterdam, where he came to discuss the matter with Hendrik Vieroot. Van Bell claimed that Ulsen gave some of the goods to him. The captain also has notarized documents made to present his case in the presence of several witnesses. Crew members testified that the captain was sober and competent during the whole voyage, in marked contrast to the chief navigator and his assistant. From later documents, dated January 9, 1769, it appears that Captain Van Bell had died, but his widow Suzanna de Heer was still suing Thomas and Hendrik Vieroot.

It appears from notarized records, that Mr. J. Beukelaar finally settled the matter of the estate on October 17, 1771, in Amsterdam. Matters were further complicated because it had to be decided what belonged to the Ulsen estate and what to the estate of the late Nicolaas Mattheus van der Nood de Gietere. Jan Pranger, former governor of Elmina Castle and custodian of his daughter Francoise, corresponded with the WIC on this matter. In the end, Jan Pranger receives eight thousand guilders on behalf of Francoise. Jan Pranger had also acted in *loco parentis* for Roelof Ulsen after his father died a year after their arrival in Elmina.

The total value of Roelof Ulsen's estate was set at ƒ115,824; and after calculations of costs, etc., ƒ112,000 was left to be divided among the heirs. This was equally divided among identified heirs on the paternal and on the maternal side. Celia Maasland, Roelof's mother's cousin, who had been destitute and dependent on the church for her upkeep, inherited two thousand florins. Out of this, she spent 510 florins to purchase a house, which still stands today. This settlement did not include Hermanus, his sister Johanna in Elmina, or the other younger African siblings or indeed their mother Adjewa Akusiba Braffoe.

Among the beneficiaries are Johanna Elizabeth Ulsen and Catharina Ulsen, the daughters of the deceased Jacobus Ulsen, who was the older brother of Jan Ulsen, the father of Roelof.

What remained after the estate was divided among the heirs was a share worth ƒ16,000. From the interest of this sum, an annual amount of four hundred guilders was to be set aside for the upkeep and education of Hermanus Ulsen until the age of twenty-two. Following the settlement of his father's estate little was heard of Hermanus until he was in his twenties. It is known from references to him in the WIC documents that he was married in the Netherlands but left his Dutch wife and returned to Elmina. It appears that the marriage was brief and unhappy.

Hermanus may have had other siblings other than his older sister Johanna. The WIC records show two other Ulsens, Jacobus and Hendrik, who may have been younger sons, deemed too young to travel when Hermanus and his father set sail for the Netherlands. They are noted as cadets or young employees of the WIC in 1774. Roelof Ulsen's relationship with Adjewa Akusiba Braffoe was a formal one since he had secured her from her owner and performed the necessary customary obligations recognizing the relationship publicly. The record on Jacobus and Hendrik is as follows:

> "Jacobus Ulsen has served his time as soldier and has left on 24 May 1775 on a commercial vessel under captain Noordhoek, to earn his living on a voyage to America. 11 dec. 1774 'Cadet Hendrik Ulsen has terminated his service 19 dec 1774' 'Cadet Hk (Hendrik) Ulsen is again serving' NBKG 141, Journaal Elmina,… mei 1775: Hendrik Ulsen has terminated his service."

Johanna Ulsen, who was freed, with her mother from slave status is also mentioned in the records in connection with a legal matter in which she was a party:

> "Today 14 february 1795 appeared before us, king, chiefs, notables, quarter representatives and the Castle council, presided over by the Hon. O.A. Duim, the tapoeyerin (mulatto woman) Johanna Ulsen on the one side, and Quassa, negro wife of the pensioned chief carpenter Frans Barteling on the other side. They presented to us their palaver, which was still undecided. We found in this case the aforementioned Quassa as well as her husband Barteling guilty of an evil fetish which was most damaging, and took into consideration the subsequent death of the hon lord Volkmar (commies J.W. Volkmar, with whom Johanna lived in a customary marriage) and many other reasons too long

to enumarate here. Therefore we have decided with the most fairness that aforementioned Quassa is wrong and that Johanna stands fully in her right and according to the custom of the land we have rendered her foufe Terre. We interdict the aforementioned Quassa and her family to engage in any acts against Johanna, under whatever pretext, and we will hold her responsible for any consequences."

Java Hill: An African Journey

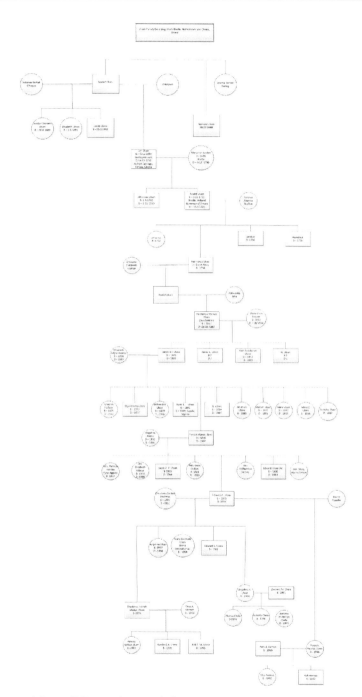

Ulzen Family Tree of Ulzens from 17th Century, Netherlands to 21st Century, Ghana

XXVII

Children born of slave women remained the property of the woman's owner until their mother's freedom is bought formally, freeing them from future servitude. Slavery in the coastal context between Africans had a complex social character. For example, Isaac Ruhle, a son of Jacob Ruhle, a wealthy Euro-African, was married to Afua Akumaba, a family slave owned by his mother Akusuwa Esson. In 1847, two days before Afua died, her owner and mother-in-law, freed her by an act of emancipation thereby ensuring that her grandchildren would officially become free persons. In another example, Elisabeth Atteveld, freed her slave Essebu by a similar deed. Both mistress and slave had borne children to Governor Frans Last. This deed ensured that all of the governor's children were ensured free status.

In 1779, Hermanus arrived at Cape Coast, the British headquarters twelve miles east of Elmina on a British pirate ship. It appeared that he had boarded this ship in Accra after having delivered a parcel to Mr. Jacobus van der Peuye, a Dutch officer in Accra.

> "The undersigned hereby declares to have received from Mr. Hermanus Ulsen, lieutenant-titulair of the Navy, in the service of the Lords of the States-General of the United Provinces [= the Dutch parliament], a letter, a golden watch and a chest marked HU no 2, which had been sent

to me by my brother Petrus van der Peuye, merchant in Middelburg.
Signed in… . Crevecoeur in Accra, 6 January 1779.
Jacobus van der Peuye."

At Cape Coast, his stated purpose of return was to visit his family in Elmina. Even though he was described as a lieutenant in the navy of the states-general when he delivered Mr. Van der Peuye's gift from the latter's brother Petrus, the WIC records refer to him as someone pretending to be the bastard son of ex-president Ulzen. Governor Woortman, who was the father of many African children who carried the surname Plange, reports,

"Some weeks ago a certain young man arrived on a British pirate ship in Cape Coast, who pretended to be Ulzen, a bastard son of the late president Ulzen. He reported to me, pretending to be lieutenant in the service of the Admiraliteit Zeeland. He said he had sailed from Holland with Captain Chastelein on whose ship he served as third officer. Capt. Chastelein has transferred him on the board the pirate ship on the Upper Coast, in order to enable him to travel to Elmina and greet his Negro family.

His arrival has surprised me. Well aware of your instructions dd. 18 oct 1774, I asked for his company passport. He said he did not need one, being a native of this place. I asked to see his permission from the Admiraliteit to leave the service and travel. He did not have one. Finally I asked him for proof that he indeed appeared in the crew register of Capt. Chastelein. He was unable to give this evidence. Then I did not hesitate to tell him that he should leave from here, the moment that Capt. Chastelein's ship will arrive here. If this ship actually arrives, I'll make sure that it takes him on board. If not, I'll send him to Europe on another ship. He is now staying in the crom (village) with his family." (WIC 434, Minutes of the Chamber Amsterdam of the WIC. 6 July 1779)

Further records reveal the racist contradictions of the WIC when they were confronted with the living results of the activities of their officers.

"'Reported is the arrival [in Elmina] of a certain Ulsen, bastard son of the late president Ulsen. This Ulsen will be sent back with the first opportunity, in accordance with the resolutions dd. 12 Aug. 1756, further specified in the resolutions of 18 Oct. 1774.'

fol. 60, 9 April 1779:

'Deliberating about the orders of the representative and governors not to take into the Company service on the Coast mulattos and tapoeyers born under company rule, this is considered by the speaker to be contrary to the Company's interest. After deliberations it has been decided to render advice to the meeting of the Heeren X.'"

Hermanus did not produce documents identifying himself and must have communicated in Dutch as to who he was, stating that he was a lieutenant on the ship commanded by Captain de Chastelain, which had sailed from the Netherlands to Dutch Accra. The same WIC records show that he was on the upper coast, in Accra as he claimed, before his arrival in Cape Coast via the British ship. Most Africans can understand clearly why he would refuse to produce any documents to reenter his own country. This retort most likely resulted from the supercilious attitude of the European officers at the port of entry. This type of interaction was probably familiar to him from his years in Holland and may have played a role in his decision to abandon his naval career in Europe.

In spite of the doubts raised about him and the supposed prohibitions to employing "children of the company," he is later employed as an assistant in the WIC at the Elmina Castle. He is later mentioned again in an uncomplimentary fashion in a poisoned pen letter undermining the Euro-African staff of the WIC. The writing of anonymous letters about Euro-African officers was apparently a common practice among the white officers who perceived the mulattos as a threat, given their natural connection to the local African population. Yet these mulattos were creations of their own passions.

"Harmanus Ulzen has become so notorious because of his behaviour in Europe that there is no need to go into details here, but your Hon can rest assured that his behaviour has not improved here on the Coast, but that he proves every day to be a fervent lover of alcohol, indeed sometimes he is already drunk at nine in the morning, and very mean and with sinister traits. This is only to be expected from someone who by his own imprudence has opted intentionally for his misfortune and who just barely escaped his well-deserved punishment on appeal. From someone who even during the first days of marriage threatened to hurt his most lovely wife, with whom many a European would have been only too happy to live in tender love, out of sheer malign hate and jealousy, only because she had danced with another gentleman." (WIC 500, OBP from de Kust van Guinea to Kamer Amsterdam, Anonymous concept missive, ongedateerd [1788]. fol. 1335.)

XXVIII

My father had been aware of the name Hermanus Ulzen as a precursor to his father's middle name Manus. He related it to someone who worked at the castle in an earlier generation, but he was unaware of Hermanus Ulzen who went to Java in 1832. This information may have been suppressed because, though service in Java had started with some Dutch-speaking mulattos and other European descendants, large numbers of slaves from the hinterland had later on overwhelmed it. This somehow made it déclassé to be a Java soldier if you were a member of the landed gentry of Elmina.

Hermanus (Manus) Ulzen, the Java veteran listed his father as Roelof Ulzen, who was a likely son of Hermanus Ulsen who worked for the WIC. There are no records available on Roelof, the putative father of Hermanus of Java and grandson of Roelof Ulsen, the former governor who died at sea. It appears he did not work for the WIC because he does not appear in their records. More importantly, by this time, the WIC had largely become defunct; and this second Roelof may well have lived initially in Holland. He was probably a son of Hermanus, born of his marriage in the Netherlands before his return to Elmina or indeed the product of a new marriage or liaison in Elmina.

On embarkation for Indonesia, Manus had stated that he had lived in Europe and was recognized by Governor Last as a Dutch-speaking *tapoeyer*. Hermanus insisted on enlisting as a corporal because he spoke Dutch and offered to act as a translator. Though he spoke Dutch, he was unlikely to speak the same language as most of the other recruits who were brought in from Ashanti. Most of these were slaves from Dagbon and other points north of Kumasi. It is possible that he lived in the Netherlands with his father Roelof and returned to Elmina for reasons that are unclear. He may also have traveled back and forth between Elmina and Holland as a seaman. The family pattern of naming supported the likelihood that Hermanus (Manus) would name his oldest son Roelof after his own father. This was, however, not the case as I discovered. His oldest son was named Jacob. The name Jacobus does exist in the genealogy of the family. Roelof Ulsen, the governor, had an uncle named Jacobus; and one of the governor's putative younger sons was named Jacobus. This person would have been a great uncle of Hermanus of Java.

The only other Ulzen mentioned on the coast is P. L. Ulzen who witnessed and probably negotiated a peace treaty in 1715. In 1714, a prominent African slave trader, Jan Conny (Dikkie Jan or Fat Jan), wanted to take revenge on a group of people called Adjase, who lived near Fort Batensteyn in Butri. They had probably been brought there by the Dutch to help in building the fort. One of these Adjase killed a rich local merchant Obim, who was a friend of Jan Conny. The Dutch tried to evacuate the Adjase to a nearby village, and some neighboring states (Wassa and Twifo) offered their assistance to the Adjase. The conflict threatened to develop into a full-fledged war, which the Dutch were anxious to avoid as it would upset trade. Finally, representatives of the two camps met in Elmina in September 1715 to sign a peace treaty. P. L. Ulzen was the witness to this peace treaty and probably also the mediator. This was well before Jan Ulsen and his son Roelof arrived at Fort San Jago. The relationship, if any, between P. L. Ulzen and Jan Ulsen is unknown. The name Ulsen or Ulzen was not an uncommon name. It is most likely that Jan Ulsen may have hailed from the town of Uelsen in the district of Grafschaft Bentheim in the state of Lower Saxony (Niedersachsen) in Germany. Most people in eighteenth century carried a surname indicating their town of origin. The other possibility is the town and district of Uelzen in the Luneburger Heide region of Lower Saxony. Uelsen is in close proximity to the Netherlands. Daniel Ulzen, my

German friend, may have had a point after all. P. L. Ulzen may have been a Brandenburger.

Manus Ulzen had settled in Elmina since his return from Java and the Netherlands and married Maria Ekua Esuon. The first of their four sons, Jacob, was born in 1845. The records show that on November 24, 1846, Manus was granted a 50 foot plot of land on the beach side of the Heerenweg to build a house. Anna Rhule, another tapoeyer was likewise granted land to build in the same year and was the first African to build a house on this site. Others granted plots to build on include Elizabeth Welzing, Betsij Abba, Atton Jan Pot and Kwamena Mijzang (Mensah) Smith. They were required to build before January 8, 1847 or their plots would be reallocated.

Manus run afoul with the law in 1854 when, along with his neighbor and fellow Java veteran Jan Pot, they accused another Elminian, Jan Niezer, of pocketing the pension payments of three Java veterans and of selling another Java veteran into slavery in Accra. Niezer was incarcerated, but the Dutch governor later determined that Ulzen and Pot had laid false charges. Ulzen was sentenced to three months in prison and a fine of sixteen dollars while Pot received a lighter sentence.

Java veterans were occasionally reengaged on brief military contracts for the Dutch administration. Between February 25 and March 31, 1868, Manus and a few Java veterans were involved in an attempt to quell an uprising by the people of Komenda, west of Elmina, who refused to hoist the Dutch flag as part of the new Anglo-Dutch territory exchange on the coast. A Dutch warship was sent to demonstrate Dutch authority along with the permanent force of the Elmina garrison and a few dozen Java veterans. "who are mostly quite willing to take up arms again to join the campaign. In spite of their advanced age, they are often very useful because of their calm courage and war experience" During this military engagement, Manus Ulzen was employed as an overseer for sick and injured soldiers. The fact that he was called in active service for five weeks indicates that he must have been in reasonably good health at the age of fifty-six.

From 1868, Manus Ulzen's name appears as cosigner on the lists of death certificates, issued by the Dutch administration. He routinely reported the death of pensioned Java veterans, signing with a cross, "having declared that he is unable to write his name." Deceased Java veterans were entitled to a coffin supplied by the Dutch administration. He had, by this time, become a leader among the free burghers and had a role to play in the deliberations regarding the impending British takeover of Elmina Castle. Dutch pension records show that he died on January 9, 1887 at the age of 75. The cause of death was not recorded in those documents.

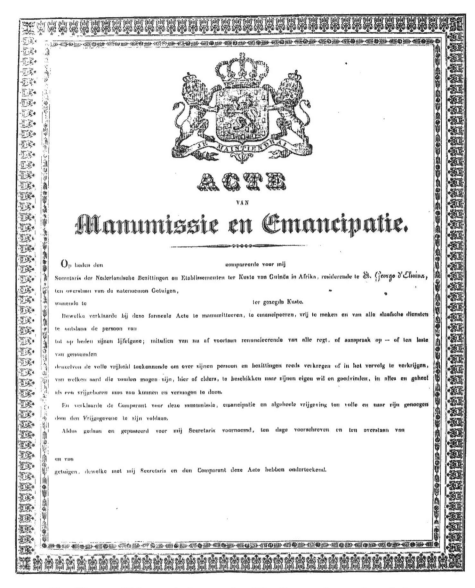

Certificate of Manumission used to "free" recently purchased slaves in Kumasi to join the Royal Dutch East Indies Army (KNIL)

Herman Daendels - Governor – General of Elmina
from December 1815 to January 1818

Manus Ulzen's Military Pension Record

An artist's depiction of a battlefield at Aceh in Java (1873)

XXIX

By 1807, the British parliament had put a stop to shipping and trading African slaves. By the second half of the nineteenth century, the abolition of the slave trade was being enforced as a sound social principle in spite of the loss to commercial interests. Emancipation Day occurred in 1863 in America. This was the political climate in which the Dutch pursued their recruitment of soldiers for Indonesia. The British authorities viewed the continued recruitment of African soldiers by the Dutch both for the East Indies and also Surinam as a covert form of slavery. This was part of the British impetus to discredit their European competitors as they aimed to consolidate and expand their interests along the coast. The Danes had already abandoned their possessions to the British, and the Dutch were the only obstacle between the British and total hegemony on the coast. This was the threshold between the end of the slave trade and the beginning of colonization, which would find Africans now uniformly suppressed and oppressed on their own land.

The British were now preoccupied with finding ways to extinguish the flame of Ashanti supremacy in the region. Elmina served as the center of the Dutch-Ashanti alliance. The recruitment of soldiers to Java and to a lesser extent, Surinam, formed a significant part of this relationship. The Ashanti Empire was at its zenith in the late eighteenth century. However, by the beginning of the nineteenth century, its southern provinces closer to the coast began to rebel, emboldened by British animus toward Ashanti. The king of Ashanti was not interested in war and sought to maintain trade in spite of the increasing British influence on the coast. The most lucrative part of the trade was in slaves, so the change in attitude toward slavery in the nineteenth century greatly undermined the Ashanti economy, which depended on the sale of captured slaves or on those acquired as tribute payments by conquered states.

In 1806, during the reign of Osei Bonsu, the British gave the rebellious chief of West Assin refuge and encouragement. They also gave refuge to the chiefs of Akim and Akwapim to the east and south, who fled to British forts on the coast for protection. The Ashanti rightly considered this a breach of long-standing diplomatic protocol, which allowed for the mutual extradition of individuals deemed to have committed crimes in their home territory. The British attempted to normalize their relationship with the Ashantis with two diplomatic missions led by Thomas E. Bowdich and later Joseph Dupuis. However, tension between the British and the Ashanti worsened with the arrival of George McCarthy, who, in 1822, began actively organizing the coastal Fanti militarily against the more powerful Ashanti. Unfortunately for him, his expedition ended tragically with his death at Asamanka near Twifo Praso, when an Ashanti detachment happened upon him quite by chance. He was beheaded and his head was sent to Kumasi to decorate a drum at the royal mausoleum. Emboldened by the death of McCarthy, Osei Yaw Akoto, successor to Osei Bonsu, continued this war, which ended badly for the Ashanti. They lost most of their administrative cadre as the British fought with Congreve rockets, new technology, which overwhelmed the Ashanti muskets.

The Fantis, now emboldened by their British allies, not only rebelled against the Ashanti but set their hungry eyes on Elmina, which was the only Ashanti stronghold on the coast. In 1831, the year before Manus Ulzen set sail for Java, a peace treaty was finally concluded under the auspices of George McLean, who had taken over at the British capital in Cape Coast. He was more interested in trade than in establishing British military supremacy in the so-called protectorates. Relative peace was maintained until his death in 1847.

Kwaku Dua ascended to the Golden Stool of Ashanti in 1834. He had benefited from the peaceful years ushered in by George McLean. He, however, had to contend with British efforts to consolidate their power along the coast as Ashanti's traditional allies, the Dutch, began to lose influence. The Danes had already sold off their assets in Accra to the British, who were determined to establish a real colony not only on the coast but also further inland. In 1852, the British introduced a poll tax, and their African allies immediately realized that British protection came with the loss of autonomy. Elmina continued to enjoy its symbiotic relationship with the Dutch and the Ashanti, but tensions and uncertainty prevailed. The British continued to give refuge to rebel chiefs from Ashanti, and in 1863, a frustrated Kwaku Dua launched a military expedition against the British to find the rebels. This was more a show of a force than a decisive military mission. In 1865, at the time of the "enstoolment" of Kobena Condua as king of Elmina, Kwaku Dua sent a letter to Cape Coast, delivered by Pieter de Heer, the Dutch consul in Kumasi, to remind the British of their treaty obligations. In this climate of impending war, Kwaku Dua suddenly died on April 28, 1867, and Kofi Karikari became king of Ashanti a month later. Pieter de Heer, who had initially accompanied the Dutch Agent from Elmina, Kwasi (Myzang) Mensah as a clerk, had stayed on in Kumasi at the request of the late king to facilitate the recruitment of soldiers for Java. He was in Kumasi when Kwaku Dua died. He provided a detailed account of the reaction of Kumasi to this event. This included a count of 1,075 human sacrifices between the death of Kwaku Dua and the enstoolment of Kofi Karikari as king of Ashanti exactly a month later. He reports, "only I go to the home of the king to look at his face as the last honour of the Netherlands Government". At this last honour he saw "the body of the king covered with gold, gold plates, surrounded by trays of gold on a gold plated bed." De Heer presented gifts to Kofi Karikari on behalf of the Netherlands government on July 29, 1867. The new king anticipated that war was inevitable since the British were intent on invading his kingdom. Though traditionally viewed as a hawk, he made numerous diplomatic overtures to the British in a bid to avoid war and increase trade.

In 1868, Kofi Karikari sent one of his senior counselors and top diplomats, Akyeampon Yaw, on a mission to Elmina. It had become clear to the people in Elmina that the Dutch would give up the castle and leave the people of Elmina to the mercy of the British. The British sought contiguous territory along the coast to consolidate their influence. Being the most powerful naval power, the British were keenly aware that the Dutch could not and would not resist them militarily. The Dutch had little to show for the 260 plus years in Elmina. Indonesia, though, was known as "Holland's milk cow" because it was by far the most profitable colonial enterprise of the Dutch, who were easily persuaded to abandon their interests in Guinea for a further consolidation of their control of Indonesia. The Dutch were ready to accept the British terms but were surprised at the intensity of the protests of local chiefs to, what in the European eyes was, a simple real estate deal or land swap.

The Dutch were already struggling in their trade as 75 percent of their goods were carried by English or American ships. The British were set to impose taxes already operational in their "protectorates." Elmina viewed the possibility of a British residency in Elmina as an infringement on her long-standing autonomy. The planned handover emboldened the neighboring Fante against Elmina, with unspoken but tacit British support. The Dutch were in no position to protect Elmina's independence, and the Ashanti were becoming increasingly worried about the future of their state.

The Dutch were already on the defensive about their recruitment of slaves from Ashanti for service in Indonesia. Since slavery had been decisively abolished, the Dutch were now engaged in an attempt to procure indentured laborers or "coolies" from India, under the aegis of the British, to serve in Surinam. They needed the British more than the British needed them. On the August 6, 1868, the chiefs and people of Elmina sent a formal petition to the Netherlands to register their opposition to the handover of the castle to the British. They received no response from The Hague. As the people became more restless in February 1869, the king sent a personal message via George Emil Eminsang (Amissah), a prominent Elmina businessman. He spoke Dutch, English, Portuguese, German, and Fanti and was the nephew the great ensign of Elmina, Kobena Eminsang.

At The Hague, Eminsang was met by a Dutch government stonewall.

It was suggested that he meet with former Elmina Governor Nagtglas. This was of course a snub of Mr. Eminsang and the message he bore for the Dutch king and parliament. Eventually, Eminsang was able to deliver his message in the appropriate forum. The hope of the Elmina government was that the Dutch would send an expeditionary force to protect them against the British tidal wave, which was about to sweep through their lives and history. The Elmina government was unaware of the inferior position from which the Dutch approached their dealings with the English.

The people of Elmina were greatly disappointed as Nagtglas was returned to Elmina as governor without an expeditionary force. Nagtglas's first attempt to establish himself was fiercely resisted in Komenda, which the British had "offered" the Dutch as part of the Anglo-Dutch agreement. There were other failures as the Dutch governor at Amanhia fled his post from similar resistance. Meanwhile, the Ashanti envoy, Akyeampon Yaw, and his party were approaching Elmina from the west. He was returning from Kumasi with over two hundred Elmina people who had attended the funeral rites of the late King Kwaku Dua I of Ashanti.

During his journey, he had taken great pains to inflict hardship on any identified enemy of Ashanti he encountered. His actions included beheadings, abductions, and other atrocities. Gov. Nagtglas felt diminished in stature with each mile that Akyeampon Yaw gained on Elmina. The stage was set for a critical confrontation between the Dutch, the king of Elmina, and the king of Ashanti represented by his Great Ensign Akyeampon Yaw. The Ashanti envoy and his party of about four hundred were welcomed in Elmina with great fanfare. There was, however, a great deal of uncertainty as many planned to flee Elmina before the arrival of the British.

Akyeampon Yaw was not the first prominent embassy of Ashanti to Elmina but historically was the most critical. The longest serving Ashanti envoy was Akyeampon Boakye who served from 1822 to 1832. His tenure ushered in a new period of stability for the Dutch-Ashanti-Elmina trade alliance. His predecessors, Fosu Kra and Gyasi, had been involved in a scandalous attempt to extort money from a son of the late Governor Daendels of Elmina.

At the ceremony to restore the tripartite diplomatic links in 1822,

Governor Last observed that though the people of Elmina were often described as "Dutch subjects" they were more "under the command of Ashanti" than himself. There is no evidence to support the notion that Elmina was subject to Ashanti. The Ashanti envoy had limited jurisdiction in Elmina territory.

Many people in Elmina were literate, and in spite of the Dutch prevarication and vagueness about the handover to the British, many were reading the discussions of these issues in the Dutch and British press. European education had been present in Elmina intermittently since the Portuguese established the first school in 1529. The Dutch had a school in 1641, which educated mostly mulatto children. It was closed for a long period and reestablished in 1850. This is probably where Manus Ulzen's children may have received their education.

On July 21, 1870, Eminsang and Kobena Gyan, successor to his father Kobena Condua as king of Elmina, confronted governor Nagtglas with their knowledge from the European press of the impending British takeover. The British were putting pressure on the Dutch to expel the king of Ashanti's envoy in an effort to rid Elmina of Ashanti influence and make it "Fanti territory." Kofi Karikari challenged the British claim to Elmina on the basis of annual payments he received from the Dutch in the form of *kostgeld*. For the first time, an African leader was questioning the presumed right of Europeans to hand over and exchange African territory between themselves. Elmina stood to lose its independence to forthcoming British taxes, a new language, and a new culture. The Europeans wanted to ascribe this resistance simply to the presence of Akyeampon Yaw. For all the years that the Dutch had been in Elmina, the king of Elmina had kept a significant portion of the economy out of Dutch reach. These included the trade in palm oil, fishing, and cattle. No cases ruled on in the king's palace could be appealed to the Dutch. In the British "protectorates," the local chiefs had diminished authority in legal matters. British civil law prevailed. Elmina's centuries-long careful diplomacy in the service of its independence as a state was coming to a frightening end.

Kobena Gyan had been thrust into the limelight in 1869 after his father Kobena Condua had been deemed pro-British. He was more likely closely aligned with the Elmina elite of businessmen and *freeburghers* (Dutch descendants). The impending arrival of the British emerged as a serious class issue in Elmina. Politically, Kobena Gyan had no choice but to represent the popular sentiment in Elmina against the British after he succeeded his father. Elmina had become a political beehive of activity with many disparate parties playing for extremely high stakes. The Ashanti envoy, the Great Ensign Akyeampon Yaw, had a garrison of troops in Elmina in support of the young king. The British were determined to eliminate the Ashanti presence in Elmina and the other grandes of Elmina, namely, the rich businessmen like George Emil Emisang, David Mills Graves, Hendrik Vroom; and the Asafo leaders were divided among themselves. They all recognized the great risk that resistance would bring on their people.

By this time, the Dutch had been forced by English pressure to detain Akyeampon Yaw at the castle to pave the way for the transfer. The young King Kobina Gyan continued to take a very hard line, informing the newly installed Governor Ferguson "that there was a rumour that the Dutch government intends to sell us to the English. We are not slaves and we do not want to see any other flag on the fort, not even on its ruins." He showed his total displeasure that his deputation to Holland had not been acknowledged with an official response and added that Elmina would oppose the transfer with arms and that whites would be among the dead. He added that known British sympathizers in Elmina would be beheaded. Furthermore, he wanted to know how much the Dutch were being paid for the transfer of a castle, which did not belong to them.

The king launched a final diplomatic mission in sending a prominent Elmina merchant, David Mills Graves, to The Hague. He also carried a secret letter meant for the Kaiser of Prussia, requesting protection or mediation from the Germans. Graves concluded an impressive mission in which he made a strong appeal in the chamber of parliament when the law concerning the transfer was addressed. He was unable to stem the tide in favor of the transfer on January 17, 1872. He left Holland for Elmina on February 1, 1872, and wrote the Dutch nation a letter of farewell in which he did not mince his words about the situation. He noted that on the orders of Minister Van Bosse, he had been watched and followed like a criminal.

After all this, the Dutch offered to pay his passage back to Elmina. He turned them down and preferred to rely on the sacrifice of the people of Elmina who had raised ƒ1,600 for his passage. He said that even though the Dutch were effectively trying to sell a free people into slavery, he would not curse them but would certainly not revere them either. After this final diplomatic failure, the Elmina bourgeoisie began to take stock and prepare for an accommodation with the English to ensure their continued prosperity as a class of people.

Manus Ulzen now a spokesman for the No. 10 Asafo Company, which was exclusively for *freeburghers,* attended a meeting called by Governor Nagtglas on March 4, 1872, to address the dispute and enforce the Anglo-Dutch agreement. At this meeting, Nagtglas asked each Asafo company to state their wishes. No. 7 as the headquarters was asked to lead, but they deferred to No. 1 Company, saying the question must be addressed in numerical order. No.1 Company, who reminded No. 7 that they were the king's quarter and should lead the deliberations, rebuffed this. The historical significance of the proceedings was not lost on Elmina's leaders. Eventually, Nagtglas decided that the companies should draw lots. The free burghers drew first, and as a result, Manus Ulzen led his team out for consultations. They returned to the gathering and, citing the destruction he envisaged would befall the town, voted to deport the Ashanti envoy Akyeampon Yaw. This cleared the way for the birth of the British flag in Elmina. This could not have been a popular decision. In spite of this, though, the other Asafo companies voted likewise after him. The stage was now set for the British takeover and the military carnage which was to follow.

As the inevitability of the British arrival became a reality, the divisions in Elmina society became more pronounced. The merchants and other members of the local bourgeoisie, some already with a good knowledge of English, began to evaluate their economic prospects. The Asafo companies represented the sentiments of the ordinary people, who entreated their young king not to cave in. However, despite Kobena Gyan's convictions and loyalty to the alliance with the Dutch, on April 6, 1872, Gov. Ferguson implemented the transfer decisively. He did this to preempt the arrival of Colonel R. L. de Haes, who had been dispatched as the king's commissioner from The Hague aboard the frigate *Admiral van Wassenenaar* with a special detachment of marines. Gov. Ferguson, on the ground in Elmina, viewed this as an affront to his honor and proceeded posthaste with the transfer. The transfer took place with much military pomp and speechmaking. The king, Kobena Gyan, had been deposed after the arrest and banning of Akyeampon Yaw in November 1871. The handover ceremonies passed without incident. No shots were fired except for the 101 gun salute for the Dutch and British flags. De Haes arrived on April 17, 1872, to a sea of British colors against the Elmina sky. Elmina was without a king.

The local bourgeoisie had tried to win their young king over, but he saw them truly as traitors to the people of Elmina. The mulatto community, including their spokesperson Manus Ulzen, the Java veteran, had opted for a second marriage with a new European suitor. On the sixth, seventh, eighth of April 1872, King Kobena Gyan refused to attend meetings at Elmina castle to discuss the hand over. After a meeting on April 26, a demonstration against the handover occurred in which Commander Joost, who was head of the Dutch transition team overseeing the mechanism for the payments of Dutch pensions, etc., was shot as he stood next to Eminsang. He died the next day. Eminsang may have been the intended target because he was viewed as having betrayed the young king. His rapid rise in profile in Hennessey's new British administration did not help matters. He was appointed to such posts as civil commandant, collector of customs, postmaster, and deputy superintendent of police. Many Africans in Dutch employ were terminated with only a month's pay and no benefits. Kobena Gyan made it clear that he would not enter the houses of traitors, whom he referred to as "those who sold my country and the country of my people for gold and place."

Eminsang could no longer function as a representative of the Dutch and was discharged from the committee on April 30, 1872. He fled Elmina where his life was in danger. He, however, worked as the acting Dutch consul in 1878 and 1879. He later became the agent for the Congo Free State and concluded an agreement in Brussels to recruit labor. For the British, he was engaged as an expert on customary law, and John Mensah Sarbah dedicated the preface of his 1897 book on customary law to him.

Of the Elmina grandes, only David Mills Graves remained loyal to the young king.

The English governor, Pope Hennessy, realized that Kobena Gyan had to be restored as king if his administration was to avoid being stillborn. Kobena Gyan was solemnly restored as king on May 8, 1872, with a seven-gun salute, to a very satisfied Elmina population. On July 22, 1872, after a trial in which four defendants in the Joost shooting case had no counsel and faced an all-mulatto jury, one man was acquitted and three executed for the murder of Commander Joost. Kobena Gyan tried in vain to prevent the execution, but the three suffered a public hanging. Elmina had attended its first meeting with British colonial justice!

Kobena Gyan had been given an English flag along with other gifts from Governor Pope Hennessy but had never flown it. His word was still law in Elmina among the ordinary folk, which disturbed the English to no end. They had to resolve the role of the king as quickly as possible. On October 28, 1872, Akyeampon Yaw was captured and brought to Cape Coast. A number of his followers in Elmina were gathered; and on December 12, 1872, he left with about four hundred followers, escorted by thirty Hausa troops in the British service. He crossed the River Pra on Christmas Day and entered Ashanti territory a broken, defeated, and disgraced man. His journey through Fanti territory had been marked by insults from the local population, now emboldened by the British, who they naively saw as allies. This day formally ended Elmina's autonomy as a state. Her carefully crafted security alliances had been devoured by the British juggernaut rolling across the Guinea coast.

Hendrik Vroom, an Elmina Grande who later became District Commissioner for the British in Tarkwa, Gold Coast in 1900

Cornelis Johannes M. Nagtglas – Governor of Elmina on 2 occasions from 1857 to 1862 and 1869 – 1871

XXXI

On March 12, 1873, at dawn, the whole Elmina government was summoned to the Palaver Hall of the castle. Only five chiefs accompanied Kobena Gyan. They were all asked to take an oath of allegiance to the English. Three acquiesced; but Kobena Gyan and two others, Tando Mensa and Kwamina Ekum, resolutely refused. Hendrik Vroom, an Elmina mulatto now in the British service, reported the king's statement as follows:

> ""The castle belonged to the Dutch government, before, and the people of Elmina were freemen; they are no slaves to compel them to do anything. When Governor Pope Hennessy came to take this castle he did not consult me before the English flag was hoisted; if he had considered me as the king he would have done so. On account of the hoisting of the English flag of the castle of Elmina the people have brought me great trouble. They have disgraced me. They themselves told me not to accept the flag. I also refused to accept the flag. Some of the people then changed their minds, and, as I would not do so, went to Gov. Ferguson and begged for ammunition to fight against me. Gov. Ferguson gave the ammunition. Gov. Ferguson then sent his colonial secretary and three other officers with a paper for me to sign. The governor offered me as a bribe a large sum of money to let that transfer go on smoothly end

peaceably. I refused the bribe because had I taken it, chiefs would have turned round on me afterwards and said I sold the country for money"

The king was then asked to take the oath of allegiance and sign a paper before him; he got very vexed and excited, struck the table with his fist and said, "I am not afraid of your power. You may hang me if you like. I will not sign any paper. I and some of the people of Elmina have taken fetish oath to oppose the English government from coming to Elmina and we have not broken that oath yet."

With that show of defiance, Kobena Gyan's fate was sealed. Along with the other two dissident chiefs, he was arrested, bundled onto the awaiting *Seagull*, and transported to Cape Coast where he was locked in debtors' jail. They were sent into exile in Sierra Leone without any charges or a trial. He arrived there on April 30, 1873, a dispirited, broken, and disappointed man. He was deeply worried about his relatives, wives, and children. He remained true to his conviction that Elmina was not to be taken and swapped between European powers at will. In 1877, four years after his deportation, his people, missing their king, petitioned the British for his return. This was granted with the proviso that he return to Elmina as a private citizen. He reasoned that he was exiled as king and rejected the terms. He thus prolonged his exile, returning to Elmina on May 17, 1898, to die. His exile lasted twenty-one years. In March 1901, he was buried at the Dutch cemetery where his soul must have found some measure of peace from the English. This was the only part of Elmina free from British imposition. The young king took a principled stand, which led to his exile by the British to Sierra Leone. He is, to this day, the most revered of Elmina's chiefs for his stand to protect Elmina's 264-year alliance with the Dutch and its independence as a state.

King Kobina Gyan after return from exile in 1898

King Kobina Gyan's Stool at his relatives' home in Elmina

King Kobina Gyan sitting in state with elders of Elmina
after his return from exile (circa 1898)

XXXII

On December 24, 1867, Jacob A. F. Ulzen, Manus' oldest son, was appointed a customs official. The purpose of the controversial exchange of territories between the Dutch and British was created to consolidate territories, to enable the European administrations to introduce a revenue system covering part of the costs of the settlements. The Dutch customs service was newly created in 1867 and staffed entirely by local officials.

Jacob Ulzen, my great-grandfather, began his career on an annual salary of 180 guilders. He was initially stationed in Butri and later in Shama then Elmina. The customs officers rotated every year to prevent familiarity with the local population, which could inhibit their zeal in collecting duties. Among his colleagues were Frederik Herman Last (on a salary of two hundred guilders), Pieter van Eijk, Jan Louis Niezer, Jan Frans Bohem, and Koffie Ernst.

Jacob's career seemed to have progressed well. In 1868, his salary was increased to two hundred guilders, and he received a bonus of thirty guilders. Subsequently, he received another increase, and on January 17, 1872, a further increase, bringing his salary up to 240 guilders. He continued in the service up till the British takeover of Elmina, living through the political strife and violence, which ensued as the new king of Elmina, the venerated Nana Kobina Gyan supported by the Ashanti, continued to resist the takeover in vain. The town of Elmina was bombarded and literally destroyed. The location of the town was then between present-day Bantuma and the castle, west of the river.

Though Kobena Gyan was gone, anti-British sentiment was still very strong in Elmina. Akyeampon Yaw had experienced a political resurrection of sorts and mounted an offensive to take St. George's Castle in June 1873. Rumors of his anticipated arrival in Elmina were rife, causing panic among the British. In early June, he was encamped at Sanka, just an hour's march north of Elmina. The locals treated his troops to rum and tobacco.

Le Jeune, the Dutch consul, reported, "It is rumoured that the Ashantis 10,000 strong are under an hour from Elmina and intend to capture fort St. George. They are busy making ladders. The Dutch flag with No:2 in the white stripe is flown by the Ashantis." Akyeampon Yaw had two sons in Elmina and had ordered his stool brought from Half-Assini to Elmina, indicating the seriousness of his intent to sit in state and hold court in the town. He had been the Debosohene or personal counselor and confidential barber of the late King Kwaku Dua. He was a patri-sibling of the late king and now needed to prove his loyalty to the new king. The die was cast.

On June 13, 1873, Elmina was placed under martial law. The castle was occupied by sixty European artillery men, one hundred or so Hausa troops; and on the Benya River, twenty armed launches and sloops with 250 men on board were positioned alongside the town, which lay west of the river. The commandant, Lt. Colonel Festing, issued a proclamation demanding that all ammunition in the town be brought to the castle. Silence. At about noon, the castle opened fire on the town, and bombs rained on Elmina from the naval ships. The Elminians who had left town later returned fire with Ashanti reinforcements, and a fierce battle ensued. They were finally subdued with the loss of about two hundred men. African volunteers in support of the British from Cape Coast then came into the town and looted and plundered it under the supervision of Col. Harley, a British official who had previously served in the town. All ancient grudges against Elmina were settled with tacit British approval.

Akyeampon Yaw had retreated to Beyin, the capital of Amanahia. By August, most of the former Dutch towns west of Elmina had been blockaded and bombarded by the British. Akyeampon Yaw was wounded during the bombardment of Beyin by the *Druid* on October 16, 1873 died soon after. Colonialism had bared its fangs and given birth to a new era on the coast. By February 1874, the Ashanti capital, Kumasi, had been set ablaze and sacked by Sir Garnet Wolseley; and the sight of an Ashanti monarch prostrating before a white man had become a new reality. The British had secured the Gold Coast, the Dutch had gained Sumatra, and the Africans had another century of oppression to look forward to as they welcomed "civilization."

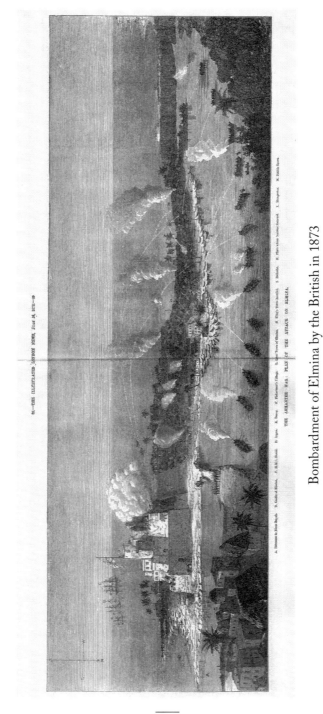

Bombardment of Elmina by the British in 1873

XXXIII

Jacob continued with his customs career in the service of the new British masters who now had complete control of the coast between Accra and Axim. He married Elizabeth Adjuah Asorbu with whom he had eleven children. He spent part of his career in Calabar, Nigeria, and eventually returned to Elmina in his retirement. Some of his children continued their lives in Nigeria where their descendants continue to live. Jacob's only written legacy is the mournful note he wrote commemorating the death of his wife on January 4, 1910. He did leave a complete list of all his children, which was eventually helpful to me in deciding that his father must have been named Hermanus. This single sheet of paper typed by Jacob Ulzen ultimately held the key to the past and pointed the way to the stories and documents that have become the complete story of the Ulzen family's evolution through the Dutch, British, and Pan-African transformations of Elmina. He appeared to be a man of strong Catholic faith who recorded not only the tragic passing of his wife in his brief family record but also the drowning death of one of his twin daughters in childhood. He noted unforgivingly that his daughter, Maattah, had died on May 28, 1895, reportedly through the carelessness of one Ms. Hayford, by drowning at the beach in Elmina, which is truly the heart of the town. She was ten years old. Jacob himself died within a year of his wife's passing.

His son, Patrick Manus, my grandfather, stayed on in Elmina after returning from Calabar, Nigeria, to bury his father. This decision kept this line of the Ulzen name in Elmina. It appears that most of the other Ulzens had moved west to Sekondi, where the growing port brought jobs to what was to become the industrial twin city of Sekondi-Takoradi.

XXXIV

We were on our way to visit my father in Nairobi, Kenya, in 1988 and were spending a few days in Ghana en route from Canada. The day before my departure for Nairobi on good old Ethiopian Airlines, I was visiting my aunt, Mrs. Mary Folson. She was somewhat somber and informed me that Papa Baffour had died the night before. Dr. R. P. Baffour had been the vice chancellor of Kwame Nkrumah University of Science and Technology at the time of Ghana's first coup in 1966. He was my father's boss and mentor. They were both fired after a commission of inquiry in 1967. Dr. Baffour was reputed to have been Ghana's first qualified engineer. He had suffered a stroke and had been bedridden for a few years. I was entrusted with the task of delivering this news to my father upon my arrival in Nairobi.

He was dressed in his trademark gray suit, readying himself for work after dropping off my daughter Adwoa and me from the airport. We had just climbed up to the first floor apartment and surprisingly found Gideon, his majordomo from years past who, as far as I had known, had long ago been laid off during the lean and mean years. This was because my father had suffered a period of unemployment after leaving the African Association of Literacy and Adult Education (AALAE) and could not afford house help. After securing a new job with Union of Radio and Television Organizations of Africa (URTNA), he rehired Gideon. My father had borne the cost of educating Gideon's children for years because he wished his children a brighter future than their father had experienced.

After all the screaming and backslapping, we settled down for breakfast. Our flight had arrived at dawn. Gideon was particularly thrilled to see my daughter. He had last seen me in 1979 while I was in Nairobi en route to Canada to secure my future as it were. I was no one's parent then. It was a brisk start to another African morning. The cars were honking as Nairobi awakened for another bustling day. Breakfast was served, and my eyes took in the new environment. My father had moved to considerably more modest digs as he gradually traveled the bumpy road toward retirement. As we ate, I pondered the issue of Dr. Baffour's death and mustered the courage to deliver the sad news immediately. Adwoa had left the table with my sister Nana to go play with the neighbor's child.

I simply remarked, almost casually that "Dr. Baffour died two nights ago." "Was it peaceful?" he asked. He made a sign of the cross, sat silently for a minute, and looked over the balcony, far into the city. He seemed to take the news well. He noted the obvious relief his friend and mentor must have gained from the years of immobility and loss of speech. He was now free from all the suffering. Later that day, I met my father at his office at the Kenyatta Conference Centre for lunch as planned. When we hit Kenyatta Avenue, he suggested we go to church. I accompanied him in near silence as we walked to the Catholic cathedral, which was empty on a weekday lunch hour. We walked through the dark heavy silence side by side, past the dark wood pews to the front row. Here, we began to say the rosary for Dr. Baffour. The Catholic Church was an all too familiar setting for any and everything in our lives. I simply accepted it as my family's denomination without question. It was more a cultural than a religious reality if you were an Ulzen. After our private observance, we walked to the Pagoda for a sumptuous meal. The soul needs food to sooth itself at such times.

XXXV

The Catholic Church in Ghana had its beginnings in Elmina. It is a story of pain, dedication, martyrdom, and eventual triumph. The early pioneers lived a near starvation existence in their mission to establish the faith in the Gold Coast. Elmina was for all practical purposes, a Methodist or Wesleyan town. Though a Catholic church was present during the Portuguese era for the mariners, this died and disappeared with the Dutch conquest and expulsion of the Portuguese in 1637.

Father Auguste Moreau arrived in Elmina from St. Helena on May 18, 1880, with Father Murat. These two French Roman Catholic priests ventured into this town, which had been under the sphere of Protestant influence for more than fifty years with literally little more than faith. They were members of the Society of African Missions (SMA), formed in 1856 and based in Lyons, France. The mission had a presence in Benin and South Africa but had chosen the Gold Coast on the recommendation of Mr. Brun, a businessman who also acted as the French consul. The climate in the Gold Coast was viewed as healthier than that of Benin. Father Moreau was thirty-three and Murat was thirty-one years old when they arrived on their mission to the newly created Gold Coast prefecture.

The priests stayed at a "rough kind of hotel" owned by George Emil Eminsang to start with and said mass there. Their two principal tasks were to acquire land for a permanent mission and to start a school to give life to the mission. This was not without serious challenges and frustrations. Father Murat succumbed to malaria in August 1880, exactly two months after his arrival and was buried at the Dutch cemetery. Father Moreau barely recovered from his earlier attacks of the same. He was afraid he would suffer the same fate and was reminded of the Catholic pioneers of Sierra Leone. In a letter to his superior, Father Planque in Lyons, he remarked, "I could not help thinking about our Saintly Founder and his companions at Sierra Leone." In spite of these fears, he left for Sierra Leone on August 15, 1880, for "a change of air" at the insistence of the doctor.

He paid a visit to the exiled king of Elmina, Kobena Gyan, and reported in detail on his melancholic state:

> "I have had the pleasure of shaking hands with the old King of Elmina, who is prisoner here. During the Ashanti war he had taken sides with them; the English have bombarded and destroyed a part of the town and taken the King to Sierra Leone as a prisoner of state. I am told the Government gives him a yearly allowance of 100 pounds. If this is so, I do not understand what he does with it for he looks as poor as Job. His home is a kind of veranda having one door, but no windows. This small hovel contains his bed, a simple mat, in one corner; in the other one a few boxes containing his belongings, I suppose; then in the middle a wooden bench. He made me sit upon it at his side.
>
> The King is of medium height, rather lean, I would say. When he speaks of his country, his eyes begin to glitter; he stammers and shakes all over his body. In the far distance he shows his land with a magnificent wave of his arm, lifting gracefully his torn cloth. 'Why have they taken my country?' he said.
>
> With him was his nephew and a few Fantis who kept him company. At the door is a policeman who, I am told, never leaves him out of sight. He came to see me at the mission."

Father Moreau returned to the Gold Coast where he had been confirmed officially as the superior of the Gold Coast mission. He requested more priests urgently and also made a plea for sisters to be sent help the school and mission in general. He planned to visit Kumasi and Accra to examine prospects for expansion even though Elmina had hardly taken root. There were few Catholics in Elmina to support the young mission. Manus Ulzen, who had apparently been baptized as a Catholic in Batavia (Jakarta), was the church keeper of the first makeshift chapel at Eminsang's hotel. He is the reason why the Ulzens of today are at the center of the church wherever they go. The other local Catholic was Mr. Nelson who was extremely helpful once land was finally found and construction crawled along. The church moved from the hotel to "Lewis House" at the foot of Java Hill. A permanent site was still sought, and requests for the Old Dutch Garden, Java Hill, and Mr. De Veer's land all came to naught. In December 1883, Father Moreau was delighted to write to his superior in Lyons that land on a hill west of Java Hill called Schomerus Hill had been acquired as the future site of St Joseph's Catholic Church. From the Lewis House, the chapel moved to Chief Krakue's house and then to the "Bridge House," where the pioneer nuns of Our Lady of the Apostles (OLA) lived.

Father Moreau administered the sacraments to the growing faithful as time moved on. He complained often of the near-starvation existence of the missionaries as he received little material support from Lyons. He wrote with great clarity of his visits to Kumasi, Axim Anomabo, and Accra and the missed opportunities lost to the financial nakedness of his mission. In his annual report to Lyons in 1885, he complained, "Father Moreau administered the sacraments to the growing faithful as time moved on. He complained often d miserable. Notwithstanding all our reports, we will not receive an additional farthing. I am discouraged."

The first church burial resulted from the tragic death of Father Murat in August 1880. During this year, five baptisms were entered in the register. The first three children baptized were mulattoes. The first marriage took place between Thomas Hamilton Steven, a British foreman of works, and Maria Anna Frederica Piquet on August 29, 1881. Two marriages were blessed on February 10, 1883. They were that of Arthur Brun, the French consular agent who assisted the priests since their arrival, and Maria Adriana Rhule and that of Manus Ulzen, the church keeper, and Maria

Ekua Esuon. The first twelve catechumens were baptized and received their first communion on Christmas Day in 1882. They were Charles Stout van Dyck, John Anquandah, Adrianus de Heer, John Andoh Kesson, Joseph Anumel, Robert Fracon, Mary Ulzen, George Mensah, Benjamin Andoh, Edward Lewis, James Villars, and James Zwennes.

Over 120 years later, the families and descendants of these catechumens continue to play leading roles in the Catholic Church of Ghana.

XXXVI

One of the highest points of Fr. Moreau's tenure though, was his visit to Kumasi in April 1882. He was impressed with the welcome he received and the assistance he received from Boakye Tenten, the prime minister and chief diplomat of the Ashanti kingdom. He was quite supportive of the idea of the Catholic mission in Kumasi. At a private meeting with the father, he produced a crucifix he kept on his person and asked for the father to bless it for him.

His account follows:

> "The arrival at Kumasi:
> On the day of arrival, they were solemnly received for nearly five hours by the Asantehene Nana Mensah Bonsu. Also Prince Boakye was present and was very kind to Fr. Moreau.
> 'On the ninth day, we were close to Kumasi, but had to wait the arrival of the messengers from the King before we could enter the capital. Next day, they arrived at 2 p.m. On 22 April 1882, we reached the house prepared for us in the city of Kumasi. Here we made ourselves ready for the public reception. As we came out, a child was standing by to show us the way. Our carriers formed a procession as we walked along a street lined by thousands of women and children

who were anxious to see the White men. Their men were on duty with their respective chiefs.

We reached a very large square, a market place, called Ediriaben. It was literally covered with people; the King and his people and a crowd of onlookers. The official party formed an immense semicircle with the King in the centre. Each chief was surrounded by his retinue also in a semi-circle; he was sitting on a chair under a large umbrella; all the other people sat on the ground. We passed along saluting with the hand, Ashanti fashion, and shaking hands with each chief. All along the line the horns were sounding and the drums beating.

We came to the King. He was on a platform, purposely made for such occasions. He was sitting in a beautiful armchair. Over the King's head about a dozen umbrellas were opened. All around him was an immense crowd of people with swords, guns, drums, horns, fans, horsetails etc. A narrow passage led to him. I am afraid I trod on many toes as I walked along the narrow passage. As we reached the King we took off our hats and saluted him. He shook hands with us. His crown resembled a Bishop's mitre in shape. Around his neck hung two heavy necklaces, one of silver and the other one of gold. His arms from the wrist to the elbow were covered with wrought gold; above the elbow other bracelets of gold were intertwined. His fingers disappeared under gold rings. His outer garment was made of golden cloth embroidered with silk of diverse colours. His sandals were ornamented with gold. His head is shaved and round, his eyes are large and glittering. He is rather small and does not look more than 40 years old. The proceedings lasted more than two hours".

Exchange of greetings:

"Another ceremony then began. We were led to the extreme end of the square to seats prepared for us. Here, we were asked to receive the King and his retinue and the chiefs and their retinues. As they passed by they saluted us. Some had only a few men, other chiefs came with many retainers, their guns, swords, drums and umbrellas. I noted in particular the war chief Kweku Finu; he was a tall and strong man with a hundred soldiers around him, guns upon their shoulders. They walked four in a row.

The fetishmen rank with chiefs; they passed before us without shaking hands. When they came to salute us they simply waved their hands and walked on. The fetish priests were accompanied by what I surmised to be novices or apprentices of their own dark art, forty or fifty young men, all dressed alike and dancing in the most extravagant manner.

When Prince Boakye came, we all stood up; he only shook hands with us, but embraced us in African fashion. It was a sign of great affection. You must know that he has married the King's mother, and in Ashanti acts as a premier or prime minister.

The King approached us next; the sound of horns, the tamtams, the shouts of the people heralded his coming. Before him marched a hundred men carrying his baggage: armchairs, stools, lamps, silver objects etc. Two articles claimed my special attention: a royal chair in ebony wrought with silver, and keys: big and small; there might have been 2.000, carried by two stalwart Ashantis. Then came the King's bodyguard of 40 or 50 men, who were, I was told, the public executioners. Their foreheads were shaved and their long hair fell in disorder upon their shoulders. Their faces are fearful especially when they dance and brandish their swords.

Then came the King. He is carried by 8 strong men in his palanquin, covered with rich draperies. All dance and clap hands. The King smiles and greets with his hand, then comes down and walks under an immense umbrella. Horsetails and fans are waved to drive flies away. The booming of the horns and drums, the shouts of the crowd go crescendo. A scene that cannot be described, so grandiose, so extraordinary. There was a moment of tense silence when the King was near us…

As we stood up to receive him, the King took my hand in his hand and held it for a long time as all the crowd cheered oh! Oh! Oh! The King performed a war dance before us first with a sword and then with a gun, and then he withdrew. Two hundred soldiers with their guns came next and finally the chiefs, forming the rear guard. At 6.30 p.m. the ceremonies were over".

That same evening several Chiefs came to see Fr. Moreau. It was past midnight before he fell asleep! The next day was a Sunday. Fr. Moreau first said Holy Mass on a portable altar. In the afternoon, he made a guided tour through the city of Kumasi.

Private Audience.

"My private audience with the King took place a few days later. Three days after our solemn audience, we went to offer our presents to the King: Mr. Brun pieces of silken cloth and myself a small harmonium which the Prince liked very much.

On 29 April, around 8 p.m., his Majesty the King sent a messenger that he wished to see us. I put on my best cassock and we went to the royal palace".

After this gracious reception, Father Moreau was further surprised by continued Ashanti hospitality. On May 6, around six in the afternoon, when Fr. Moreau was taking his meal, Prince Boakye arrived in haste, telling them that the king wanted to see them. They followed Prince Boakye to an immense marketplace where they were invited to sit down. Fr. Moreau reported:

> "A strange sight met our eyes. A long train of people in single file were coming from the Palace *(Ahenfie)* towards us. At their head marched the chief sent by the King and Prince Boakye. They greeted us and waited till those carrying the presents had arrived. At a given sign those in front stopped. A servant carrying a golden plate came to Boakye and handed over to him, one by one, the small packets with gold powder.
>
> Prince Boakye addressed the man and said: "Interpreter, tell the White Men that these are the presents of the King: to the White Man here 6 ounces of gold; to the priest

('Asofo') 4 ounces of gold'; and so was done for every item. There was a cow for Mr. Brun, a pig for me, two sheep, one for each of us, fowl, ducks, eggs, ground nuts, palm nuts, pine apples, bananas, yams, all borne by a hundred and fifty carriers at least. They went to our house where they put down their loads. A huge crowd of curious spectators lined the road on both sides of the procession".

Father Moreau's observations continued:
"We see a clear indication of the Asantehene's preference: Mr. Brun was the more important visitor of the two. We will come back to this. Fr. Moreau was, nevertheless, very pleased. After his return to Elmina, he wrote to Fr. Poirier, the SMA Procurator at Lyons on 30 June 1882:
"I am sending you a copy of my sketchbook. It represents Prince Boakye offering us the King's presents.
I wrote in my diary on 7 May:
On our return yesterday, we found in a corner of the yard a mountain of bananas etc. Mr. Brun will take his cow to Elmina; there are already too many pigs at Elmina. I shall have it killed this evening.
(The following day) The pig is dead. We have kept a piece for ourselves and given the rest to our carriers and the landlord of the house we stay in. We have made a general distribution of yams, plantains, groundnuts etc."

Fr. Moreau and Mr. Brun stayed three weeks at Kumasi. Before leaving the Ashanti capital, they went to say goodbye to King Mensah Bonsu and Prince Boakye.

They reached Elmina on 18 May 1882, having covered on foot the whole Ashanti road, passing Kokofu, Bekwai, Fomena, Praso, Foso, Manso, Abura Dunkwa, Abakrampa, 156 miles up and 156 miles down to Elmina.

Father Moreau returned to Elmina after this glorious visit, but unfortunately, the mission in Kumasi did not become a reality until a lot of turmoil had transpired through the Ashanti kingdom.

In 1884, Prince Boakye Tenten was killed after his opposition to the new king, after the king, Mensah Bonsu, was destooled. In 1896, the year the young King Prempeh I was deported to the Sechyelles, a Basel mission opened in Kumasi; and the Catholic Church did not come until 1910, twenty-eight years after Father Moreau's historic visit and twenty-four years after his death.

From its early beginnings in Elmina, the Catholic Church has had many devoted Ulzens in its fold. This commitment to the Catholic Church has lived with the Ulzen family to the current generations. My father's older brother, Jacob Abraham Fredrick Ulzen, Master Ulzen to most, was the principal of the Catholic school in Elmina during his lifetime; and my father Edward was a widely acclaimed Catholic choirmaster wherever he lived in Africa. His youngest sister, Mary Ekua Esuon Folson, a music educator by vocation, is very active in the music of the church to this day. Having taken for granted the role of Catholicism in the family, we had no knowledge that the seeds of the fruits of Catholicism were sown in faraway Indonesia with the baptism of Manus Ulzen, the old soldier and first church keeper in Elmina. His third son Bart followed him in this role and was the godfather of many of the early Catholic children baptized in Elmina.

XXXVII

My father, Edward Abraham Kofi Ulzen, was born on Friday February 15, 1926. He was the fifth of eight children in this pioneer Roman Catholic family of Elmina. He was educated in Catholic Infant and Primary Schools until 1938 when he entered St. Theresa's Seminary to study for the priesthood. He left the vocation in 1941 and proceeded to St. Augustine's College from where he graduated in 1943 with a Grade 1 Cambridge Senior Certificate. The principal, Fr. Maurice Kelly, referred to him in his written testimonial as "an intelligent and refined young man."

He started work as a pupil teacher at the Roman Catholic School at Dunkwa-on-Offin in 1944 but left to join the colonial civil service in HM Customs and Excise as a second division officer. He was initially stationed in Takoradi, where he later became active as an organizer of the new Convention People's Party (CPP). He chartered the first branch of the youth wing of the party. These young men were later popularly known as the "verandah boys" who propelled the CPP to power. As a result of these activities, the British authorities transferred him to Cape Coast, which did not have a real harbor. Officers had to sail out to sea, over the boisterous waves, to inspect incoming ships. On one of these trips, the canoe in which he was travelling in capsized. He almost drowned because he was clothed in his full uniform; he could not swim! He was saved by the skilled oarsmen or *asankwafo*. After this near-tragic accident at sea, he finally decided to stop carousing around town and heed the advice of his mentors, Kwame Nkrumah, Mr. Budu Atta (later Nana Kobina Nketsiah, Omanhene of Essikado, Sekondi), and Mr. Bredu-Pabi, to further his education.

He had been a student of Mr. Nkrumah, who was head teacher of the St. Joseph's Catholic School, Elmina, for a year in 1931 and later taught for three years at St. Theresa's Seminary. He was one of the children who received extra tutoring in the evenings from the man, who was later to lead the Gold Coast to independence in 1957. As a customs officer, my father was one of the first Gold Coasters to welcome Kwame Nkrumah and Kojo Botsio back home as their ship docked in Takoradi on December 16, 1947. His vision of the future was inseparable from the Pan-African dream, which grew out of the struggle for independence.

He entered the University College of the Gold Coast in 1950, where he studied history and completed his post graduate studies in education in 1956. He reentered the Ghana Civil Service as an education officer in Ashanti, Northern, Upper, and Brong-Ahafo regions. While in Wa in the Northern Region, Dr. Nkrumah, as prime minister, paid a visit. He requested that my father be eventually transferred to Accra where he continued his career as an assistant secretary for education in the Office of the President during the first republic.

As administrative secretary to the National Universities Commission, he played a central role in establishing the Kwame Nkrumah University of Science and Technology (KNUST). Others like Dr. E. A. K. Edzii became registrar of the University of Ghana; and J. H. K. Folson, later to become his brother-in-law, worked on establishing the University of Ghana Medical School and proceeded to a very successful career in the Ghana Civil Service, retiring as a senior principal secretary for finance.

My father became interim secretary of the University Council, and later, the first registrar of the newborn KNUST. He was dismissed from this position in 1967, following a politically motivated commission of inquiry after the first military coup in 1966, which toppled the government of Dr. Kwame Nkrumah.

In August 1967, he joined the faculty of the University of Zambia (UNZA) as a senior lecturer in extramural studies. This was the beginning of his career in East, Central, and Southern Africa. He later became the first black African registrar of UNZA at the invitation of President Kenneth Kaunda. He ushered in a new era, leading the way for Africanization of the university and established statutes, regulations, and by-laws for governance of the young institution. In 1972, he went on to become registrar of the University of Botswana, Lesotho, and Swaziland (UBLS) Examinations Council in Maseru, Lesotho. After a year in this role, he became the registrar of UBLS itself. Again, he was the first African in such a senior administrative position. He began to recruit qualified Africans to faculty positions and eventually wrote the statutes establishing the National University of Lesotho when UBLS was devolved into three separate national universities.

In 1977, he moved to Nairobi, Kenya, to establish a permanent secretariat for the African Adult Education Association (AAEA). He transformed this fledgling organization into the largest literacy organization in the world through relentless international fund raising and his tireless spirit. He accomplished this through mergers with smaller organizations and by fostering the formation of national adult education associations across Africa, out of which, African Association for Literacy and Adult Education (AALAE) was created. In 1986, he left AALAE and began work initially as a consultant then later as project coordinator for the Family Health Broadcast Programme of the Union of National and Television Organizations of Africa (URTNA). In 1989, he was Africa's representative at the World Bank NGO Forum.

He retired from URTNA in 1992 and returned to Ghana in 1993. Soon after his return to his native land, he developed a significant cardiac illness, which limited his activities. In spite of these limitations, he served on the task force to establish the Roman Catholic University in Sunyani and was later appointed chairman of the board of the Bureau of Ghanaian Languages, a position of service to his nation he held at the time of his passing. Throughout his life, he remained passionate about his children, education, Africa, and Catholicism. He was a musician of note, conducting Catholic choirs wherever he lived. He was also a thespian and quite simply a scholar in the truest sense of the word. He was a fatherly mentor to many academics, professionals, and leaders of this generation of Africans.

Edward A. Ulzen and his son Dr. Thaddeus Ulzen in Toronto (1992)

Edward A. Ulzen assisting at Catholic Validation Service of marriage of Thaddeus & Ekua Ulzen (1992)

Edward Ulzen with his sons Thaddeus and Edward Stephen in Toronto (1992)

Edward Ulzen with his first grandson and namesake Kweku Edewar Abram at his baptism in Toronto (1992)

Edward and Christiana Ulzen with Adwoa, their first grandchild, Toronto 1983

His father, P. M. Ulzen, was a civil servant who served in difl parts of the Gold Coast and Ghana. He worked in the judicial service as a court interpreter. He was a man of precision in his affairs and was generally thought of as determined and uncompromising. He was a soldier in his own way. His children, though, were more involved in education and the war against illiteracy. Edward Ulzen epitomized this mission of his generation of Ulzens. The Ulzens had started off from the Netherlands as soldiers with the arrival of Jan Ulsen in 1731.They had generally been administrators; soldiers; and, on occasion, leaders in their communities. In the bicultural Euro-African world of Elmina, they straddled leadership positions in both worlds. They were never wealthy people but always did an honest day's work as it was defined in each era of history covered by the ten generations of the family in Elmina.

My father Edward embodied the qualities of leadership, hard work, simplicity, discipline, and the love of the simple things in life like music and the traditions of Elmina. Every generation has been involved in public service, which for some included military service. One thing remains constant through the ten generations covered in this story: the Ulzens have always traveled beyond their visual boundaries to make new lives for themselves. From Jan, through the Roelofs and Hermanuses, it is rare to find an Ulzen who simply stayed put in Elmina. For every generation, though, someone returned to replant the name and confront the challenges defined by the times. This generation, like the last one, has continued to identify education as its mission. We have accepted a mission to preserve Elmina's history and to engage in philanthropic projects for this old city-state that is still our souls' home. If there were only a word or two to remember our father by, it would be that he was a most generous man. He was in love with conversation all his life but never referred to anything he did for anyone. People from all strata of society often informed us about his generosity and kindness. Many times, we benefited from "retaliatory" kindness from people who wished they could have reciprocated his generosity in some way. I was very surprised to find out from Dr. Ineke van Kessel in an e-mail dated March 19, 2002, that "Father Jan van Brakel (the retired missionary who first alerted me to Bart Ulzen), told me that your father, when registrar of KNUST in Kumasi, made a donation that paid for the construction of the road uphill to the St. Joseph Church in Elmina." I shouldn't have been surprised. Not only was he generous, he believed deeply in the work of the Catholic Church.

When I was about sixteen, I received admission letters to the University of Rochester, New York, and the University of Pennsylvania. I was quite proud of myself and was sure that I was on my way to the United States for my university education. My father listened carefully to my plans and dreams then finally offered his firm opinion. He congratulated me on my academic success but said he believed that every child of his should at least complete his or her first degree in an African university. He felt strongly that if the institutions he had helped create were not good enough for his own children then his work had no meaning. This kind of conviction is hard to find these days, when many leaders of governments in Africa have diminished the contributions of their universities and have sped their unprepared children to the West for a seemingly brighter future. This pattern of behavior has been a particular hallmark of the military regimes of the last two decades, which robbed many African countries of the social values and principles which were to guide their development.

We have decided to sustain Edward Ulzen's boundless generosity and love of knowledge by establishing the Elmina-Java Museum so that, through eternal conversations about Elmina's history, we will contribute to the advancement of knowledge, health, and education in this our beloved and ancient town.

Of Edward's children, our homes have been in countries our father took us; but we also charted our own journeys beyond the three hills of Elmina, determined by our own realities. The children of African independence have become the children of exile. We have lived collectively in the USA, UK, Canada, South Africa, Botswana, and Ghana at various times as adults. Most of us are engaged in public service of some sort regardless of our primary professional interests and training.

I am reminded of an old gentleman from Elmina who was a laboratory technician at Korle Bu Teaching Hospital where I trained. He would call out to me from time to time as I crossed a street on the campus. "Hey Ulzen!

You want to be a doctor, eh? You will end up being a teacher whether you like it or not." He considered my name synonymous with public education.

We await the journeys of our descendants but always remember that Elmina is our home and is indeed the center of the history of the modern world for those who know and understand the forces which propelled Africans to travel the world by force. For the Black Dutchmen, there was an appearance of choice, but they had to fight for their lives in Indonesia to eventually taste freedom. The millions of Africans who were captured, sold, and forcibly transported across the Atlantic to the Americas and the Caribbean had no such option to exercise their yearning for freedoms lost.

In researching this aspect of my family history, I was most enlightened and touched by the predicament of Kobina Gyan, the young king of Elmina, who was really the last man standing between freedom and the oncoming freight train of British colonialism. His deeply felt convictions and his loyalty to the ordinary people of Elmina are the values of leadership which are so difficult to find in Africa these days. His Ashanti contemporary, Kofi Karikari, has often been depicted as an unrepentant warrior; yet he applied great diplomatic skills in attempting to save his kingdom from the inevitable. He raised fundamental questions about the rights of Africans in their own land, for which the British had no credible answers. He actually showed that he was guided mostly by the principles of a true statesman in handling the complex challenges of his time. As my daughter Adwoa put it, "I think Manus Ulzen was on the wrong side." I would have to agree.

Adwoa contributed more to this story than her incisive opinion of her distant ancestor, Manus Ulzen. She became quite enthralled by the process of tracing this line of the family tree and was in the final year of high school when this quest begun. By the time I attended the Belanda Hitam reunion in Rotterdam, she had decided to research the story as her final school project.

She traveled to the Netherlands in December 2000 on her first major journey alone, and with the help of Dr. Van Kessel and Natalie Everts, she continued the search from where I had left it in the fall. She visited Brielle and met with Arie van Zoest, the amateur historian who had kept the life story of Roelof Ulsen alive long enough for his African descendants to find it. He said he knew that one day his African descendants would arrive, and his faith did not disappoint him. He added to the family tree, which had ended with its European branches stunted in the 1700s. He lived long enough to see the story he had nurtured all his life become a reality with the arrival of an African girl seeking her own story. Adwoa was interviewed by *Rotterdam Dagblad* on her paradoxical journey as an African seeking her European roots. She had to answer questions no one ever asked Roelof Ulsen about his involvement in the slave trade. Her answer is now part of the public record.

On a later mission to Ghana in 2004, she spent some time tracking down Kobina Gyan's descendants to find out what they remembered of their ancestor. They still possessed a photograph of the king, which they refused to part with at any cost. When in passing, she mentioned his grave in the Dutch cemetery; they told her that he was never buried there. "Where is he then?" she asked. "Right where you are," they said. "Where?" "You are sitting on the king" was the answer. He has been with his family all these years, never to be exiled again.

It will take an archeological dig to confirm this. It is, however, most likely that he was buried right in his family home, given the circumstances of his life. I thought he was at peace in the Dutch cemetery, but come to think of it, would he not find the greatest peace by being at home forever?

Adwoa Ulzen and Aire van Zoest at Archives in Brielle, Netherlands in 2000

Adwoa Ulzen with van Zoest at the Archives in Brielle, Netherlands, in 2000

Kobina Gyan's Grave – Acknowledged final resting place of King Kobina Gyan at the Dutch Cemetery in Elmina

Old Dutch Cemetery in Elmina

XXXVIII

We learn many lessons from the past which, hopefully, guide us all to a better future for our people and ourselves. The stories told here remind us of why our ancestors always live with us in Africa. Their victories are ours to keep; their errors may continue to blind us, but the stories of our own lives will become the ancestral stories of future generations. The children of independence who became the children of exile will return and rebuild from their broken stories of flight, immigration, and the distorted freedoms and customs of other lands. These are our days, so in our time, shall Africa truly exceed its great potential as a great continent of free nations? The irony of Africa is that it is the birthplace of humanity, yet its people are still fighting for freedom. How did that happen?

Others younger than ourselves and many yet unborn will tell their own stories in their own time. The greatest legacy of our ancestors from one generation to the next was the inspiration to face the challenges of their times and accomplish their appointed purposes in the service of humanity. In the end, the lessons of history provide us a better path to the future if we seek it with diligence.

Belanda Hitam (Black Dutchmen) descendants led by Daan Cordus 3rd from left, at Elmina Castle on their pilgrimage to attend the official opening of the Elmina – Java Museum in 2003

Java Museum sign – man modeling uniform of African conscripts for Royal Dutch East Indies Army (KNIL) in front of Elmina - Java Museum in Elmina.

Java Hill: An African Journey

Elmina Java Museum, opened to the public on February 15, 2003

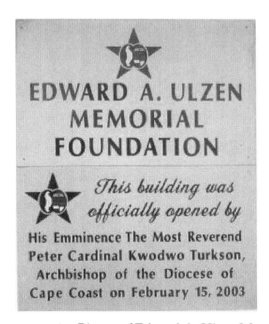

Commemorative Plaque of Edward A. Ulzen Memorial Foundation at Elmina – Java Museum

Dr. Van Kessel speaking at opening of Elmina –
Java Museum on February 15, 2003

Thaddeus Ulzen (Author's) Family Portrait USA 2009;
Standing: L-R Kweku and Adwoa;
Sitting: L –R Thaddeus, Ekua and Kofi.

Epilogue

This manuscript sat fermenting slowly over a period of about ten years after it served its cathartic purpose for the author and those who were invited to read it. In this span of time, two of Edward Ulzen's successors as head of the Nyanyiwa family of Elmina have crossed the river to meet him at the village.

The venerable Supreme Court judge, His Lordship Justice Charles Hayfron-Benjamin, is gone; but before he did, he eagerly attended the commemoration of the Edward A. Ulzen Memorial Foundation on February 15, 2003, in Elmina. He accepted his customary bottle of Scotch malt and told me in good humor as he departed for Kumasi that because of his advancing age, he would drink it slowly but surely at one teaspoon a day. He expressed his pride at how his uncle had been immortalized by the establishment of the foundation.

Mr. Mensah was not in his window overlooking the street when I got to Elmina a few seasons ago. The retired headmaster had been slowly fading away last year but still welcomed his whisky. His eyes had grown dim, and sadly, he was not able to succeed the judge before he was called up. It now falls on our generation to carry the torch and contribute effectively to the development of our country and continent for the benefit of the many underprivileged and poor who are still trying to find a path to true emancipation.

INDEX

A

Aacht, 3

Abakrampa, 159
Abesi, 96
Abocan, 96
abrofo, 75
Abura Dunkwa, 159
Accra, 2, 8, 13, 23, 29–30, 32–34, 43, 51, 54–55, 73, 78, 88, 116–18, 122, 129, 147, 153, 162
adinkra, 56
Adjase, 121
Adjaye, Elizabeth, 48, 71
Adjaye-Fraiku, Robert, 24
Admiral van Wassenenaar, 136
Afful, 25
Africa, 1, 5, 10, 18, 21, 32, 42, 47, 49, 53–54, 58–59, 61, 74, 78–79, 82–85, 88–89, 103, 105, 109, 149, 151, 160, 163, 168–69, 173
African Adult Education Association (AAEA), 32, 71, 163
African Association of Literacy and Adult Education (AALAE), 149, 163
Aikins, Angelina, 16, 47

Aikins, R. R., 47
Akan, 14, 16, 29, 37, 40, 48, 75–76, 90, 96, 98
Akim, 95, 128
Akodee Turom, 3
Ako Sika, 48
Akotex Foundation, 20
Akrampafo, 97
Akumaba, Afua, 116
Akwapim, 128
Akyem, 89, 97
Allade, 96
Amakuma, Maame, 47
amanee, 3, 7, 37
Amba, 96
Americas, 169
Amissah, J. K., 16
Amsterdam, 78, 81, 86, 102, 111–12, 117, 119
Andafo, 89
Andoh, Benjamin, 154
Andrews, Elizabeth, 30
Andrews, John, 24
Anona, 97

Anquandah, John, 154
Anumel, Joseph, 154
Apakanmuba, 48
Arhin, 23
Asafo companies, 25, 80, 97, 134–35
Asafo No. 1 Company, 135
Asafo No. 7 Company, 25, 41, 97, 135
Asafo No. 10 Company, 80
Asamanka, 128
Asantehene, 66, 155
Asante Kotoko, 30
Ashanti, 40, 56, 58, 62, 66, 80, 89–90, 96, 121, 127–35, 137, 143–45, 155–56, 158–59, 162, 169
Ashanti-British wars, 40
Asorbu, Elizabeth Adjuah, 147
Atlantic, 1–2, 6, 12, 110, 169
Atta, Abbenada, 56
Atta, Budu. *See* Nketsiah, Nana Kobina
Atteveld, Elisabeth, 116
Austin, Ato, 24
Austin (master), 24
Axim, 18, 50, 104–5, 147, 153

B

Baesjou, Rene, 80
Baffour, R. P., 149
banku, 35
Bantama, 2
Barteling, Frans, 113
batakari, 80
Batavia, 55, 60, 153
Batensteyn, Fort, 121
Bekwai, 159
Belanda Hitam (Black Dutchmen), 74, 76, 80–83, 169
bendas, 89–90
Benin, 151
Benya River, 2, 144

Berij, 110–11
Beyin, 144–45
Big Mama, 33, 47–48, 71
Boakye, Akyeampon, 131
Boakye, Kwasi, 62
Bohem, Jan Frans, 143
borebore, 34
Botsio, Kojo, 162
Botswana, 32, 163, 168
Bowdich, Thomas E., 128
Braffoe, Adjewa Akusiba, 112–13
Braffoe, Aquisiba Adjewa, 107
Brandenburgers, 21, 49
Bredu-Pabi, 162
Brempong, 44
Bridge House, 153
Brielle, 87, 108, 169
British Customs, 25
British Parliament, 127
Brun, Arthur, 153
Bureau of Ghanaian Languages, 34, 163
Burgomaster, 97
Burkina Faso, 81, 85
Busia, Kofi Abrefa, 86
Butri, 2, 121, 143

C

caboceers, 90–91
Calabar, Nigeria, 25–26, 50, 147–48
Canada, 14, 33, 83, 149–50, 168
Canadian Airlines, 35
Cape Coast, 2, 10, 12–13, 16, 24, 81, 95, 116–18, 128–29, 137, 140, 144, 161
Cape Coast Regional Hospital, 10
Cape Coast University, 13
Cape of Good Hope, 60
Caribbean, 169

castle, 1–2, 19, 54–56, 80, 83, 87, 95–96, 98, 103–4, 108, 112–13, 118, 120, 123, 130, 134, 139, 144
Catholic Church, 9–11, 16, 55, 150–51, 153–54, 160, 168
Chapel Square, 6
Christ the King Church, 43
Clara Henrietta, 59–60
Clement, Anthony, 73
Clerck, 52
Codjoe, Joanna, 12
colonial civil service, 161
Condua, Kobena, 129, 133
Conduah (chief), 7
Conny, Jan, 121
Conny, John, 96
Convention People's Party (CPP), 161
Coopstad & Rochussen, 107, 111
Coopstad, Herman, 111
Corantier, 91
Cordus, 5, 75, 81, 83, 85–86

D

Daan Cordus, 81, 83
Daendels (governor), 131
Dagbon, 85, 121
Dagomba, 90
Daily Graphic, 24
DANAFCO, 20
Daniel Ulzen, 49–50, 121
Datsun, 12
de Haes, R. L., 135
de Heer, Adrianus, 154
de Heer, Pieter, 67, 129
de Heer, Suzanna, 112
De Jonge Adriana, 61–62
delegatien, 59, 66–67
De Muralt (colonel), 61
Denkyira, 89, 96

Detroit, 78
Dikkie Jan, 121
Doortmont, Michel, 73
Druid, 145
Dupuis, Joseph, 128
Dutch, 3, 5, 18–19, 21, 25, 40, 47–49, 51–56, 58–60, 62, 65–67, 76, 79–80, 82–84, 86, 89–90, 95–99, 102–3, 110, 113, 116, 118, 120–23, 127, 129–36, 140, 143–45, 147, 151–53, 170
Dutch and Belgian Archives of West Africa, 54
Dutch Archives of West Africa, 53
Dutch Cemetery, 3, 47–48, 99, 140, 152, 170
Dutch East Indies, 5, 54–55, 59–62, 66–67, 85, 127
Dutch East Indies Army (KNIL), 54, 60, 67, 82–83
Dutch Guinea, 58, 86, 102
Dwumo, 89

E

Ebusuapanyin, 14
Edina, 2, 20
Edzii, E. A. K., 162
Eijniakon, 91
Eijnin, Kweku, 91
Ekua, 35, 37, 39, 52
Ekum, Kwamina, 139
Elet, Oppercommies, 88
Elmina, 1–2, 5, 8, 10–12, 16, 18, 24–25, 29–30, 40–41, 47–51, 54–56, 58–62, 65–67, 73–75, 79–80, 82–83, 85–91, 95–99, 102–5, 112–13, 116–18, 120–23, 127–37, 139–40, 143–44, 147–48, 151–53, 159–62, 167–69, 177

Emancipation Day, 127
Eminsang, Kobena, 130
Eminsang (Amissah), George Emil, 130
English, 39, 73, 79, 130–31, 134–35, 137, 139–40
Enkuizen, 53
Enyampa, 96–97
Erasmi, Peter, 104–5
Ernst, Koffie, 143
Essebu, 116
Esson, Akusuwa, 116
Esuon, Maria Ekua, 74, 122, 160
Everts, Natalie, 86, 169

F

Fanti, 19–20, 25, 29, 37, 39, 89, 96, 128, 130, 133, 137
Fat Jan. *See* Conny, Jan
Ferguson (governor), 134–36, 139
Festing (lieutent colonel), 144
Flagstaff House, 43
florins, 59, 61, 105, 112
Folson, Araba, 39
Folson, J. H. K., 162
Folson, Mary, 33, 37, 149
Fomena, 159
Foso, 159
Fosu Kra, 131
Fracon, Robert, 154
Francisca, 15
French, 39, 95, 151, 153
fugu, 80
Fynn-Aggrey, Johanna, 54

G

Germany, 21, 49–50, 121
Ghana, 2, 5, 19, 21, 23, 25, 29, 32–35, 44, 49–52, 54, 70, 78–81, 83, 85–86, 88, 95, 149, 151, 154, 162–63, 167–68, 170
Ghana Civil Service, 81, 162
Ghana Medical School, 33, 162
Ghansah, 37
Gietere, Nicolaas Mattheus vander Noot de, 89–90, 97, 110, 112
GIHOC Pharmaceuticals, 20
Glenfiddich, 38
Gold Coast, 2, 80, 89, 95, 145, 151–52, 162, 167
Golden Stool of Ashanti, 129
governor, 1, 61, 79, 83, 86, 89, 96–98, 102–6, 110, 112, 116, 118, 120–22, 131, 133, 137, 139
Grafschaft Bentheim, 121
grandes, 90–91, 134, 137
Graves, David Mills, 134, 137
Groot Vaandrig, 97–98
Guevara, 19
guilders, 54, 61–62, 104, 109, 111–12, 143
Guinea, 52, 58, 65, 86, 88, 102, 110, 119, 130, 137
Gyan, Kobena, 133–37, 139–40, 144, 152
Gyasi, 131

H

Haley, Alex, 85
Harderwijk, 60–61
Harley (colonel), 144
Hausa, 137, 144
Hayfron-Benjamin, Charles, 37, 75, 177
Hearts of Oak, 30
Hennessy (pope), 136–37
HM Customs and Excise, 161
Hogenboom (governor), 1

Holland, 50, 53, 60, 80, 83, 104–5, 108–10, 117–18, 120–21, 130, 134
Hollywood Hotel, 51
Huydecoper, Balthasar, 102
Huydecoper, J. P. T., 102–3

I

India, 15, 87, 89, 130
Indo-European, 56, 84
Indonesia, 58, 60, 65, 67, 75, 80, 82–84, 120, 127, 130, 160, 169

J

Jakarta, 55, 60, 153
Java Hill, 2, 5, 10, 56, 65, 153
Java War, 58
Joanna, 12, 16
Johanna, 7, 29, 54, 107, 112–14
Joost (commander), 136–37

K

Kaneshie, 23, 51, 55, 70
Karikari, Kofi, 129, 133, 169
Kaunda, Kenneth, 163
Kelly, Maurice, 161
kente, 56, 80
Kenya, 32, 149, 163
Kesson, John Andoh, 154
king, 43, 50, 58, 66, 89–90, 96–98, 113, 128–31, 133–37, 139–40, 143–44, 152, 155–59, 169–70
Kloekenaar, D., 108
Kokofu, 159
Komenda, 96, 122, 131
Korle Bu Teaching Hospital, 168
kostgeld, 98, 133
Kotoka Airport, 24
Kraba, Nana, 16
Krakue (chief), 153

Kumasi, 11, 24–26, 34, 62, 65–67, 80, 85, 121, 128–29, 131, 145, 153, 155, 158–60, 168, 177
Kunta Kinte, 85
Kwaku Dua I, 62, 80, 129, 131, 144
Kwame Nkrumah University of Science and Technology (KNUST), 20, 26, 29, 34, 44, 70, 149, 162, 168

L

La Coragie, Lord, 87
Lampong, 60
Lans (governor), 66
Last, Frans, 59
Last, Frederik Herman, 143
Latin, 39, 73
Legon Hall, 19
Leiden, 86
Lesotho, 19–20, 32, 71, 163
Lewis, Edward, 154
Lower Saxony, 121
Luneburger Heide, 121
Lusaka, 11, 34, 56, 88
Lyons, France, 151–53, 159

M

Maasland, Celia, 112
makelaar, 95–96
malaria, 152
Manso, 159
Manus-Ulzen, Thaddeus Patrick, 19
Marowafo No. 9 Company, 97
Mary, 15, 33, 36–37, 39, 74, 149, 154, 160
Maseru, 11, 19, 163
McCarthy, George, 128
McLean, George, 128–29
Mensa, Tando, 139
Mensah, A., 20

Mensah, George, 154
Mensah, Mansa, 7, 42
Mensah Bonsu, 155, 159
Methodist Church, 3, 6
Middle Temple, London, 71
Miltz, 105
Mohammed, 16
Moreau, Auguste, 151–53, 155, 158–60
Mother's Inn, 23, 44
Murat (priest), 151–53

N

Nagtglas (governor), 131, 133, 135
Nairobi, 11, 32–33, 71, 149–50, 163
National Archives, 47
National university of Lesotho, 71, 163
Netherlands, 5–6, 50, 54–56, 59–60, 67, 74–76, 78, 80–82, 102–3, 105, 108, 111, 113, 118, 120–22, 129–30, 167, 169
Niedersachsen, 121
Niezer, Jan Louis, 122, 143
Nketsiah, Nana Kobina, 162
Nkrumah, Kwame, 162
Nortey, Ernest, 20
North Carolina, 30, 78
Nova Scotia, 33
Nsona, 97

O

Obim, 121
Obodum, Kwasi, 90
Odesola, S. O., 50
Ohen, 96, 98
Okyeame, 75
Old Dutch Garden, 153
Omaboe, Edwin, 51
Opoku Ware I, 90
Oppercommies, 88

Osei, 30
Osei Bonsu, 128
Osei Kojo, 89–90
Osei Yaw Akoto, 128
Our Lady of the Apostles (OLA), 153
Oyster Bay Hotel, 5

P

Pagoda, 150
Palace Close, 23, 36, 70
Papa Annan, 15
Papa Mends, 18
Paris, 5
Passop, Pieter, 95
Patricia, 30, 33, 70, 72
pen and contract, 97–98
Peuye, Jacobus van der, 116–17
Phillips, H. H., 33
Pichem. *See* Berij
Piquet, Maria Anna Frederica, 153
Plange, 117
Planque (priest), 152
Poku, Kwame, 62
poll tax, 129
Porter (archbishop), 24
Posuban Shrine, 3
Pot, Jan, 122
Pra, River, 137
Pranger, Jan, 87–88, 112
Praso, 159
Publicola, 108–10
Purowerajo, 66

Q

Quainoo, Ebo, 36, 51
Quammena, 96
Quow Mysang, 96

R

Raems, Penni, 104–5
Ravesteijn, 105
Regiment Nationalen, 87
Requiem, 16
Rhule, Anna, 122
Rhule, Maria Adriana, 153
Robertus Hendrikus, 67
Roman Catholic, 37, 43, 151, 161, 163
Roman Catholic Cemetery, 43
Roman Catholic University, 163
Roots, 85
Rotterdam, 107–11, 169–70
Rotterdam Dagblad, 170
Rotterdams Walvern, 67
Ruhle, Isaac, 116
Ruhle, Jacob, 116

S

Saint Amant and Wolterus, 87
Sakyi, Nana Asante, 30
San Jago, Fort, 96, 121
Sanka, 144
Sarbah, John Mensah, 136
Scandinavian, 50
Schiedam, 80, 82
Schomerus Hill, 153
Schoon Verbond, 60–61
Seagull, 140
Sefwi-Wiawso, 50
Sekondi, 18, 25, 50, 148, 162
Sekyi, Adwoa, 7
Semarang, 66
Sierra Leone, 140, 152
slave trade, 40, 59, 95, 103, 107, 127, 170
Sluijter, Hendrik, 111
Society of African Missions (SMA), 151, 159
Sokko, 81
Solo, 66
South Africa, 151, 168
Sprogel, Jan, 104
St. Anthony, Fort, 104
St. Augustine's College, 10, 13, 81, 161
Steenberg, 109
Steven, Thomas Hamilton, 153
St. Helena, 151
St. Jago Hill, 2, 87
St. Joseph's Hill, 2
St. Theresa's Seminary, 161–62
Student Movement for African Unity, 18
Sumatra, 60, 82, 145
Surinam, 96, 98, 108–9, 127, 130
Swaziland, 32, 163
Sybil, 16, 25, 29, 54–55, 75

T

Takai, 85
Takoradi, 2, 29, 36, 148, 161–62
tapoeyer, 56, 59, 120, 122
Tekki, 96
Tenten, Boakye, 155, 159
Tetteh, 29–30
Texel, 60
37 Military Hospital, 8, 33
Tonnebjer (governor), 61
Toronto, 20, 23, 32
Twifo, 89, 121, 128
Twifo Praso, 128
Two Hearts of Kwasi Boachi, 80

U

Uelsen, 121
Uelzen, 121
UK, 20, 33, 71, 83, 168
Ulsen, Catharina, 112

Ulsen, Jacobus, 112–13, 121
Ulsen, Jan, 87–88, 112, 121, 167
Ulsen, Johanna Elizabeth, 112
Ulsen, Johannes, 87
Ulsen, Roelof, 86–87, 89–91, 97–98, 102–5, 107–13, 120–21, 169–70
Ulzen, Angelina, 16
Ulzen, Bart, 54–55, 167
Ulzen, Edward Abraham Kofi, 10, 20
Ulzen, Eliyah Herm, 53
Ulzen, Elizabeth Asorbu, 26
Ulzen, Georgius Rodolfus, 74
Ulzen, Heindrik, 61
Ulzen, Henry, 74
Ulzen, Herman, 50
Ulzen, Hermanus, 52, 74, 76, 79, 97, 120
Ulzen, Jacob A. F., 26, 50, 55, 74, 143, 147
Ulzen, Manus, 15, 24, 55, 59–62, 66–67, 74, 76, 80, 83, 87, 122, 128, 132, 135–36, 153, 160, 169
Ulzen, Mary, 154
Ulzen, N., 74
Ulzen, Nanabanyin Edward, 97
Ulzen, Patrick Manus, 15, 24, 76, 87
Ulzen, Patrick Manus, Jr., 50
Ulzen, P. L., 121–22
Ulzen, Rodolfus, 74
Ulzen, Roelof, 56, 79, 120
Ulzen, Swait, 74
Ulzen, William Frederick, 50
Ulzen-Appiah, Francis, 15
Ulzenhiemers, 50
Ulzen-Mile, 50
Union of Radio and Television Organizations of Africa (URTNA), 149
United States, 8, 32, 39, 86, 168
University of Botswana, Lesotho, and Swaziland (UBLS), 163
University of Ghana, 19, 50, 162
University of Ghana Medical School, 162
University of Lesotho, 71, 163
University of Pennsylvania, 168
University of Rochester, New York, 168
University of Zambia (UNZA), 162–63
Utrecht, 61

V

Van Bell (captain), 109, 111–12
van der Peuye, Jacobus, 116–17
Van der Puije, 117
van Dyck, Charles Stout, 154
Vandyke, Jacob, 98
Vandyke, Peter, 47–48, 98
van Eijk, Pieter, 143
van Kessel, Ineke, 5, 54–55, 74–76, 78–80, 82–84, 86–87, 167, 169
van Keulen, Cecilia, 87
van Keulen, Maria, 87
van Mensburg, Jacoba, 52
van Tets, L. Jacob, 104
van Ulsen, Hermanus, 19
van Velsen (doctor), 56
van Wassenenaar (admiral), 136
van Zoest, Arie, 87, 108, 169
Verbeet, Gerardus, 103
Verveer, Jan, 62, 66–67, 80
Vieroot, Hendrik, 112
Vieroot, Johannes, 87, 111–12
Villars, James, 154

W

Wa, 81, 162
Wailing Wall, 44
Wassa, 89, 121

West India Company, 87, 89
Wilhelmina, 3, 15
Willem I, 61
Wolseley, Garnet, 145
Woortman (governor), 117
World Bank NGO Forum, 163
Wuijster, Leendert, 109

Y

Yacoba, 29
Yamoransa, 29

Yaw, Akyeampon, 130–31, 133–37, 144
Yorke (master), 25

Z

Zambia, 32, 56, 162
Zeeland, 53, 117
Zevenhuizen, 87
Zuiderzee, 60
Zurich, 32
Zwennes, James, 154

Additional Sources

1. Cherchez la Femme
   Gender – Related Issues in Eighteenth – Century Elmina
   Natalie Everts: Itinerario, European Journal of Overseas History, Vol. XX, 1, 1996
2. West African Coastal Slavery in Nineteenth Century: The case of Afro-European Slaveowners in Elmina
   Larry Yarak: Ethnohistory 36:1 (Winter 1989)
3. Africans and Europeans in West Africa: Elminians and Dutchman on the Gold Coast During the Eighteenth Century
   Harvey M. Feinberg, Transactions of the American Philosophical Society, Vol. 79, Part 7, 1989
4. New sources for the study of slavery and slave trade: Dutch Military Recruitment in Gold Coast and Asante, 1831 – 72
   Larry Yarak: Source material for studying the slave trade and the African Diaspora, Centre for Commonwealth Studies, University of Stirling, Occasional Paper Number 5, December 1997
5. African mutinies in the Netherlands East Indies; A nineteenth – century colonial paradox
   Ineke van Kessel: In "Rethinking Resistance: Revolt and violence in African History Ed; Jon Abbink, Mirjam de Bruijn & Klaas van Walraven, 2003
6. Indo-African Communities in Java in Merchants, Missionaries and Migrants: 300 years of Dutch-Ghanaian Relations
   Ineke van Kessel and Endri Kusruri, Amsterdam 2002
7. Two Hearts of Kwasi Boachi

Arthur Japin London, 2001

8. Labour migration from the Gold Coast to the Dutch East Indies: Recruiting African Troops for the Dutch Colonial Army in the age of indentured labour.
Ineke van Kessel in Fractures and reconnections: civic action and the redefinition of African political and economic spaces: ed. by J. Abbink 2012
9. An Asante Embassy on the Gold Coast: The mission of Akyeampon Yaw to Elmina 1869-1872, *René Baesjou African Social Research Documents Vol. 11 1979*
10. Van Brakel, Jan SMA, The first 25 years of SMA missionary Presence in the Gold Coast (1880 – 1905) Nimègue 1987 – The Catholic Church in Ghana 1880 – 1905.
11. Dr. Ineke van Kessel – personal correspondence (2003-2005)and documents from the Dutch Archives, Den Haag
12. Aire van Zoest – Genealogy of Ulzen and van Keulen Families of Brielle, Holland (Personal papers) – 2000.
13. Oral interviews – Mrs. Mary Folson (Accra, Ghana), Dr. Francis Ulzen – Appiah (Kumasi, Ghana), Johanna Fynn- Aggrey in Elmina, Ghana.